*To: Ar
With best
healthy retirement,
to help!
Gary*

A SIMPLE GUIDE TO YOUR
RETIREMENT INCOME

JUSTIN E. GARRISON, JR. (GARY)

This document discusses general concepts for retirement planning, and is not intended to provide tax or legal advice. Individuals are urged to consult with their tax and legal professionals regarding these issues. This handbook should ensure that clients understand a) that annuities and some of their feature have costs associated with them; b) that income received from annuities is taxable, and c) that annuities used to fund IRAs do not afford and additional measure of tax deferral for the IRA owner.

Copyright © 2014 by GPS All rights reserved. No part of this publication may be reproduced, distributed, or transmitted in any form or by any means, electronic or mechanical, including photocopying, recording, or by any information storage and retrieval system, without written permission of the publisher, except in the case of brief quotations embodied in critical reviews and certain other noncommercial uses permitted by copyright law.

Printed in the United States of America

First Printing, 2014

Gradient Positioning Systems, LLC
4105 Lexington Avenue North, Suite 110
Arden Hills, MN 55126
(877) 901-0894

TABLE OF CONTENTS

ACKNOWLEDGMENTS i

INTRODUCTION 1

CHAPTER 1: DEFINING YOUR GOALS 7

CHAPTER 2: THE COLOR OF MONEY 21

CHAPTER 3: CREATING AN INCOME PLAN 29

CHAPTER 4: UNDERSTANDING SOCIAL SECURITY 35

CHAPTER 5: MYTHS AND REALITIES OF ANNUITIES: FILLING THE INCOME GAP 51

CHAPTER 6: EARNING MONEY BY SAVING MONEY: UNDERSTANDING RETIREMENT INCOME TAX 67

CHAPTER 7: THE BRANDEIS STORY 79

CHAPTER 8: THE FUTURE OF U.S. TAXATION 89

CHAPTER 9: THE IMPACT OF VOLATILITY ON THE INDIVIDUAL INVESTOR 103

CHAPTER 10: YELLOW MONEY AND YOUR RETIREMENT 109

CHAPTER 11: NEW IDEAS FOR INVESTING 123

CHAPTER 12: PREPARING YOUR LEGACY 127

CHAPTER 13: YOUR LEGACY BEYOND DOLLARS AND CENTS 141

CHAPTER 14: CHOOSING A FINANCIAL PROFESSIONAL 147

GLOSSARY 165

ACKNOWLEDGMENTS

First, I would like to thank my wife Megan for always encouraging me to be my best. To my parents for their endless love, and to my children who inspire me every day. Finally, I would like to thank Nick Stovall, Mike Binger, Nate Lucius and Gradient Positioning Systems, LLC for their contributions to this project.

INTRODUCTION

George and Dee are tired of losing money in the stock market. As a married couple in their early 70s, they can't put off retiring any longer, nor do they want to. George worked 48 years with MN Power and his wife, Dee, was an elementary school teacher. At the end of 2007, they had collectively saved 1.3 million dollars in mutual funds and stocks. But by the end of 2010, their account value dropped to just under $950,000. George and Dee felt a $350,000 hit was pretty significant, but the only advice they got from their stockbroker was, "Hang on! The market will always come back."

Well, George was 73 and his wife was 72. They didn't have time to "hang on." They couldn't wait for the market to come back, and they don't want to ride the roller-coaster of the stock market any more. They want to protect what they have, and get out while the getting is good. But the pressing concern foremost in their minds is, will they have enough to retire on after losing so much money?

Today's retirees absolutely have a right to be concerned. Retirement isn't like it used to be with a gold watch, guaranteed pension, and comfy armchair come age 65. Times have changed. Many people retiring in the new millennium are still paying off their homes, struggling to cover the rising costs of college tuition for their kids or health care for themselves. A lot of people are tightening their belts during retirement, or heading back out into the workplace because the income is just not there. Contributing factors include fewer and fewer companies offering pensions, a decline in the number of companies offering 401 (k)s, and the new timeline structure for Social Security, requiring people to wait longer before drawing on their benefits. And as if that isn't enough, people are also living longer today than they were 30 years ago.

Most people have an idea of how much money they need to retire with, but they don't know how they're going to get it. They can list out the expenses, and the bills; they know how much they owe and what they own. But they don't know how to stretch their income to meet their short-term and projected long-term needs.

In the last 25 years, retirement has gotten more stressful and more demanding, with more of the responsibility for accumulating, protecting, and managing those hard-earned assets is placed squarely on YOUR shoulders. Don't wait until the day after you retire to start thinking about where your income is going to come from. If you are one of the many individuals riding the biggest retirement wave the US economy has ever seen, this book is designed to give you the information you need to negotiate the fickle tides of retirement waters.

THE PARADIGM SHIFT OF RETIREMENT

How you approach your retirement years directly affects the amount of money you'll have to work with. **The worst mistakes often come from doing the right things at the wrong time.** Not waiting long enough to take your Social Security benefits, paying too high an income tax on your assets, and appropriating a disproportional amount of assets in high-risk, high-growth accounts all directly impact the security of your financial future.

Retirement requires a complete shift: you go from growing your money, to managing your money. Once you retire and are no longer working, you can't build that money back up. It's time to factor in how to protect what you've accumulated. A lot of people wait until disaster strikes before making this paradigm shift, and as a result, they lose money. Switching into a management mind- set gives you the peace of mind and freedom to enjoy the retirement you deserve.

THE ROAD MAP TO FINANCIAL SUCCESS

Wealth is a holistic concept. It relates not only to monetary or financial interests, but also to happiness, health, relationships, faith and peace of mind. Several of the words used to define wealth go hand-in-hand with other aspects of our life, and these aspects can actually complement one another. If you have your finances in order and you know where your retirement income is coming from, the peace of mind that knowledge brings leads to less stress, better overall health, and the ability to get more enjoyment out of these golden years.

Finances can be the largest source of stress for a family, but with a planful approach to retirement, they can also become a source of joy. The road map to financial success begins with accumulation, but it doesn't end there. A simple approach to retirement can be boiled down to these three words:
- Accumulate
- Protect
- Transfer

You've worked hard to **accumulate** your money. Take care of it now so it can take care of you. Manage your wealth by turning on your income streams at the appropriate times, and moving that money into balanced portions of red, yellow and green-money (defined in the upcoming chapters of this book) managed accounts that **protect** your assets, so more income can be available to finance your chosen lifestyle. Once this income is secured, the next step is to **transfer** the remaining wealth to your heirs or favorite charity, in the most tax efficient way possible, so you can keep more of what you've earned. If we can accomplish all three of these objectives, then we've covered the spectrum.

A successful retirement is one that you can enjoy without stress. Having a plan helps take away the worry of where your income is coming from, whether or not your money is safe, based on your risk tolerance, whether it is earning enough to sustain your desired income stream, and what portion is subject to tax. The roadmap to a successful retirement as outlined in this book takes you through the following:

Defining Your Goals. Because you want a retirement plan that's as individual as you are, we start with your questions and most pressing concerns. A financial professional can help you identify solutions to your problems by assessing the security of your assets. Separating the hope-so money from the know-so money reveals the plan or strategies required to achieve your retirement goals.

Creating An Income Plan. Retirement is funded by pensions, Social Security checks, and money withdrawn from IRAs. If there are any gaps between the money you want to have and the money that you are getting, then we take a look at your other assets and revise an income plan using those assets the most efficient way possible.

Managing Your Money. Moving your money into a calculated balance of protected and growth-focused accounts is an essential step when moving into the retirement stage of your life. The right kind of annuities can often be used to accomplish both goals, providing a relatively safe solution to fill in any income gaps while also growing a portion of your money for profit. This helps ensure that you don't just keep up with inflation, but continue to potentially generate growth in preparation for unforeseen health care costs, funeral costs, and the legacy you want to leave behind for loved ones.

Saving in Taxes. One way to keep more of your retirement income intact is by effectively managing your wealth so it is taxed at the lowest rate possible. This strategy allows you to earn more by saving more.

Creating a Legacy. Because your wealth encompasses more than just the dollars and cents you leave behind, working with a financial professional is vital to creating a lasting legacy. Having both you and your spouse present at these meetings keeps you both in the know when it comes to identifying your wishes for leaving a legacy and understanding important financial documents.

Finding a Financial Professional. Working with a financial services professional to help you craft your retirement takes away the tendency to rely on assumptions when it comes to investment and retirement planning. We need more facts. Assumptions can lead to mistakes; but facts rarely do. If you take the time to sit down with a professional and look at the numbers, you'll find there's little gray area. That's what Retirement Investment Advisors do for their clients. We replace the assumptions with knowledge and facts so you can make accurate decisions that do more than just pad your wallet - they bring you peace of mind.

On a more personal note, the information presented to you here is more than just a simple plan for retirement. It's the foundation of the same investment strategies I practice myself. One of the most surprising key pieces in the planning of retirement has nothing to do with the money we keep, and everything to do with the money we choose to give away. And I have a story I'd like to share with you about that:

My wife and I decided a few years ago that we wanted to start giving back to the community. We selected an organization called Project Zero as our first charity. In Little Rock, there are over five hundred kids in the foster care system with no real place to call home, and no one to call family. The mission of Project Zero is to match one foster child with one family until there are zero foster children in the community. That year we hosted their annual Christmas party, and three children were placed through adoption into families that had been waiting and hoping to adopt a child. We found this experience both exhilarating and inspiring, and it set things into motion. Two years ago, my wife and I stood in the parking lot of a Panera Bakery, looking at the photo of two foster children, brother and sister. Without even hesitating, we decided to adopt them. Lucy and Shepherd are ages 7 and 5 respectively this year, and we are proud to call them our own.

When people hear this story, they often remark how lucky the children are to have landed in our home. And we have to tell them, oh no, we are the ones who have been blessed.

While everybody has different beliefs, there's a universal realization that comes as you approach the end of your life. Whether the end comes when you are old, or not as old as you'd like, it brings with it the knowledge that life isn't about how much money we make, or how much stuff we own. It's about the difference we make in people's lives. And that's why I have the particular passion that I do. It is my sincere desire to help you plan for a retirement that gives you the freedom to express the difference you want to make.

Justin E. Garrison, Jr. (Gary), Investment Advisor Representative

1
DEFINING YOUR GOALS
"What do you want your retirement money to do for you?"

Will your Social Security benefit, 401(k) savings and other retirement assets be enough to provide you with the means to accomplish the things you always dreamed of doing during your retirement years? If you're like Gary and Marie, you hope so. When the couple turned 60 years old, they started thinking about what their lives would be like in the next 10 years. When would they retire? What would their retirement look like? How much money did they have?

They could both count on Social Security benefits, but neither one really knew how much their monthly checks would be, or when to file for them. Gary had a modest pension that he could begin collecting at age 67. He had always hoped to retire before that age. Marie had a 401(k) she regularly contributed to, but she honestly wasn't exactly sure how it worked, when she could draw money from it, and how much income it would provide once she retired.

While Gary and Marie might sound like they're totally in the dark about their retirement, the truth is there are a lot of people just like them. They know retirement is coming and know they have some assets to rely on, but they aren't sure how it will all come together to provide them with a retirement income.

You spend your entire working life hoping that what you put into your retirement accounts will help you live comfortably once you clock out of the workforce for good. The key word in that sentiment and the word that can make retirement feel like a looming problem instead of a rewarding life stage, is hope. You hope you'll have enough money.

Leaving your retirement up to chance is unadvisable by nearly any standard, yet millions of people find themselves hoping instead of planning for a happy ending. With information, tools and professional guidance, creating a successful retirement plan can put you in control of your financial management.

QUESTIONS ABOUT RETIREMENT

Defining your retirement goals starts with a series of questions. Most people do something to plan for retirement, but they don't often take the time to sit down and ask the questions.

What do you want your money to do for you? Answers vary for each individual, and include examples such as: "I want to pay off my mortgage." "I want my wife and me to be able to travel extensively." "I want to fund my grandchildren's education. "I want to give back to a church, charity or other civic organization."

Once we define what's important to you, we can talk about what steps you have taken so far to reach these goals. **Do you feel like you're on track right now to reach your desired goals?** If so, great! We can then move into sharing what those thoughts and strategies are. If the answer is no, then we take a look at what can we do specifically to help you reach those goals.

Most people are not on track. There is a certain percentage that are, but by and large, the majority of people aren't where they'd like to be. They might be able to retire, yes, but may fall short of being able to implement all of their goals. Reasons for these shortcomings include the loss of retirement funds in the stock market, not starting to plan for retirement early enough in life, and unexpected expenses, such as having to take care of a special needs child.

Sometimes life circumstances can derail even the best of intentions. Meeting with a financial professional can help you get back on track. Most people find they have a much greater peace of mind after meeting with a financial professional than they do when thinking about their future in "hope-so" terms.

How Much Money Do You Need? While this amount will be different for everyone, the general rule of thumb is that a retiree will require 70 to 80 percent of their pre-retirement income to maintain their lifestyle. Once you know what that number is, the key becomes matching your income need with the correct investment strategies, options and tools to satisfy that need.

When Do You Need Your Money? If you need income to last 10 years, use a tool that creates just that.

To take the "hope" out of retirement and replace it with a "know" requires a management of your risk. A tool used to identify what percentage of your assets should be at risk is known in the financial planning world as "the rule of 100." This rule takes a look at the appropriate amount of risk based on your age. The next step is to organize your separate assets based on their risk factors. We do this by using a color chart known as "the color of money." This tool will give you a clear picture of how you are currently set up for retirement income. After determining your income amounts and their sources, we reach the third stage: identifying the gaps. If there is a shortfall – and most people discover that there is – we can provide options which can potentially fill those gaps. When you take health care costs, potential emergencies, plans for moving or traveling, and other retirement expenses into account, you can really give your calculator a workout. You want to maximize retirement benefits to meet your lifetime income needs. A financial professional can help you identify strategies and customize an income plan that helps you achieve your desired retirement goals.

NEW IDEAS FOR RETIREMENT

Advice about what to do with money has been around as long as money has existed. Hindsight allows us to see which advice was good and which advice didn't cut the mustard. Some sources of advice have been around for a very long time. While there are some basic investment concepts that have stood the test of time, most strategies that work adapt to changing conditions in the market, in the economy and the world, as well as changes in your personal circumstances.

The reality is that investment strategies and savings plans that worked in the past have encountered challenging new circumstances that have turned them on their heads. The Great Recession of the early 2000's highlighted how old investment ideas were not only ineffective but incredibly destructive to the retirement plans of millions of Americans. The dawn of an entirely restructured health care system brings with it new options and challenges that will undoubtedly change the way insurance companies provide investment products and services.

Perhaps the most important lessons investors learned from the Great Recession is that not understanding where your money is invested (and the potential risks of those investments) can work against you, your plans for retirement and your legacy. Saving and investing money isn't enough to truly get the most out of it. **You must have a planful approach to managing your assets.**

Essentially, managing your money and your investments is an ongoing process that requires customization and adaptation to a changing world. And make no mistake; the world is always changing. What worked for your parents or even your parents' parents was probably good advice back then. People in retirement or approaching retirement today need new ideas and professional guidance.

HOPE SO VS. KNOW SO MONEY

Let's take a look at some of the basic truths about money as it relates to saving for retirement. There are essentially two kinds of money: *Hope So* and *Know So*. Everyone can divide their money into these two categories. Some have more of one kind than the other. The goal isn't to eliminate one kind of money but to balance them as you approach retirement.

Hope So Money is money that is at risk. It fluctuates with the market. It has no minimum guarantee. It is subject to investor ac- trinity, stock prices, market trends, buying trends, etc. You get the picture. This money is exposed to more risk but also has the pop- entail for more reward. Because the market is subject to change, you can't really be sure what the value of your investments will be worth in the future. You can't really *rely* on it at all. For this reason, we refer to it as Hope So Money. This doesn't mean you shouldn't have some money invested in the market, but it would be dangerous to assume you can know what it will be worth in the future.

Hope So Money is an important element of a retirement plan, especially in the early stages of planning when you can trade volatility for potential returns, and when a longer investment timeframe is available to you. In the long run, time can smooth out the ups and downs of money exposed to the market. Working with a professional and leveraging a long-term investment strategy has the potential to create rewarding returns from Hope So Money.

Know So Money, on the other hand, is safer when compared to Hope So Money. Know So Money is made up of dependable, low-risk or no-risk money, and investments that you can count on. Social Security is one of the most common forms of Know So Money. Income you draw or will draw from Social Security is guaranteed. You have paid into Social Security your entire career, and you can rely on that money during your retirement. Unlike the market, rates of growth for Know So Money are dependent on 10-year treasury rates. The 10-year treasury, or TNX, is commonly considered to represent a very secure and safe place for your money, hence Know So Money. The 10-year treasury drives key rates for things such as mortgage rates or CD rates. Know So Money may not be as exciting as Hope So Money, but it is safer. You can be fairly sure you will have it in the future.

Knowing the difference between Hope So and Know So Money is an important step towards a successful retirement plan. People who are 55 or older and who are looking ahead to retirement should be relying on more Know So Money than Hope So Money.

Ideally, the rates of return on Hope So and Know So Money would have an overlapping area that provides an acceptable rate of risk for both types of money. In the early 1990s, interest rates were high and market volatility was low. At that time, you could invest in either Hope So or Know So Money options because the rates of return were similar from both Know So and Hope So investments, and you were likely to be fairly successful with a wide range of investment options. At that time, you could expose yourself to an acceptable amount of risk or an acceptable fixed rate. Basically, it was difficult to make a mistake during that time period. Today, you don't have those options. Market volatility is at all-time highs while interest rates are at all-time lows. They are so far apart from each other that it is hard to know what to do with your money.

Yesterday's investment rules may not work today. Not only could they hamper achieving your goals, they may actually harm your financial situation. We are currently in a period when the rates for Know So Money options are at historic lows, and the volatility of Hope So Money is higher than ever. There is no overlapping acceptable rate, making both options less than ideal. *Because of this uncertain financial landscape, wise investment strategies are more important now than ever.*

This unique situation requires fresh ideas and investment tools that haven't been relied on in the past. Investing the way your parents did will not pay off. The majority of investment ideas used by financial professionals in the 1990s aren't applicable to today's markets. That kind of investing will likely get you in trouble and compromise your retirement. Today, you need a better PLAN.

HOW MUCH RISK ARE YOU EXPOSED TO?

Because money is so hard to earn, ask yourself, why would you want to put any more of it at risk than you have to? Many investors don't know how much risk they are exposed to. Organizing your assets according to their level of risk alerts you to areas where your investments might be vulnerable. Identifying these potential losses *before* they happen is the key to a planful retirement approach. This process starts with identifying the two kinds of money.

Hope So Money, as the name suggests, is money that you *hope* will be there when you need it. Hope So Money represents what you would like to get out of your investments. Examples of Hope So Money include:
- Stock market funds, including index funds
- Mutual funds
- Variable annuities
- REITS

Know So Money is money that you know you can count on. It is safer money that isn't exposed to the level of volatility as the asset types noted above. You can more confidently count on having this money when you need it. Examples of Know So Money are:
- Government backed bonds
- Savings and checking accounts
- Fixed index annuities
- CDs
- Treasuries
- Money market accounts

> » Ben had a modest brokerage account that he added to when he could. When he changed jobs a couple years ago, at age 58, Ben transferred his 401(k) assets into an IRA. Just a few years from retirement, he is now beginning to realize that nearly every dollar he has saved for retirement is subject to market risk.
>
> Intuitively, he knows that the time has come to shift some assets to an alternative that is safer, but how much is the right amount?

RULE OF 100

Determining the amount of risk that is right for you is dependent on a number of variables. You need to feel comfortable with where and how you are investing your money, and your financial professional is obligated to help you make decisions that put your money in places that fit your risk criteria.

Your retirement needs to first accommodate your day-to-day income needs. How much money do you need to maintain your lifestyle? When do you need it?

Managing your risk by having a balance of Hope So Money vs. Know So Money is a good start that will put you ahead of the curve. But how much Know So Money is enough to secure your income needs during retirement, and how much Hope So Money is enough to allow you to continue to benefit from an improving market?

In short, how do you begin to know how much risk you should be exposed to? While there is no single approach to investment risk determination advice that is universally applicable to everyone, there are some helpful guidelines. One of the most useful is called *The Rule of 100*.

The average investor needs to accumulate assets to create a retirement plan that provides income during retirement and also allows for legacy planning. To accomplish this, they need to balance the amount of risk to which they are exposed. Risk is required because, while Know So Money is safer, more reliable and more dependable, it doesn't grow very fast, if at all. Today's historically low interest rates barely break even with current inflation. Hope So Money, while less dependable, has more potential for growth. Hope So Money can eventually become Know So Money once you move it to an investment with lower risk. Everyone's risk diversification will be different depending on their goals, age and their existing assets.

So how do you decide how much risk your assets should be exposed to? Where do you begin? Luckily, there's a guideline you can use to start making decisions about risk management. It's called the Rule of 100.

THE RULE OF 100

The Rule of 100 is a general rule that helps shape asset diversification* for the average investor. The rule states that the number 100 minus an investor's age equals the amount of assets they should have exposed to risk.

---

* *Asset Diversification disclosure – Diversification and asset allocation does not assure or guarantee better performance and cannot eliminate the risk of investment loss. Before investing, you should carefully read the applicable volatility disclosure for each of the underlying funds, which can be found in the current prospectus.*

The Rule of 100:
100 - (your age) = the percentage of your assets that should be exposed to risk (Hope So Money)

For example, if you are a 30-year-old investor, the Rule of 100 would indicate that you should be focusing on investing primarily in the market and taking on a substantial amount of risk in your portfolio. The Rule of 100 suggests that 70 percent of your investments should be exposed to risk.

$$100 - (30 \text{ years of age}) = 70 \text{ percent}$$

Now, not every 30-year-old should have exactly 70 percent of their assets in mutual funds and stocks. The Rule of 100 is based on your chronological age, not your "financial age", which could vary based on your investment experience, your aversion or acceptance of risk and other factors. While this rule isn't an ironclad solution to anyone's finances, it's a pretty good place to start. Once you've taken the time to look at your assets with a professional to determine your risk exposure, you can use the Rule of 100 to make changes that put you in a more stable investment position — one that reflects your comfort level.

Perhaps when you were age 30 and starting your career, like in the example above, it made sense to have 70 percent of your

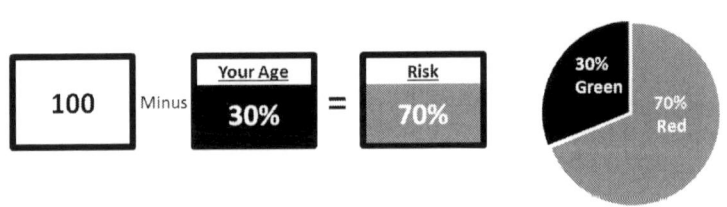

money in the market: you had time on your side. You had plenty of time to save more money, work more and recover from a downturn in the market. Retirement was ages away, and your earning power was increasing. And generally, younger investors should take on more risk for exactly those reasons. The potential reward of long-term involvement in the market outweighs the risk of investing when you are young.

Risk tolerance generally reduces as you get older, however. If you are 40 years old and lose 30 percent of your portfolio in a market downturn this year, you have 20 or 30 years to recover it. If you are 68 years old, you have five to 10 years (or less) to make the same recovery. That new circumstance changes your whole retirement perspective. At age 68, it's likely that you simply aren't as interested in suffering through a tough stock market. There is less time to recover from downturns, and the stakes are higher. The money you have saved is money you will soon need to provide you with income, or is money that you already need to meet your income demands.

Much of the flexibility that comes with investing earlier in life is related to compounding. Compounded earnings can be incredibly powerful over time. The longer your money has time to compound, the greater your wealth will be. This is what most people talk about when they refer to putting their money to work. This is also why the Rule of 100 favors risk for the young. If you start investing when you are young, you can invest smaller amounts of money in a more aggressive fashion because you have the potential to make a profit in a rising market and you can harness the power of compounding earnings. When you are 40, 50 or 60 years old, that potential becomes less and less and you are forced to have more money at lower amounts of risk to realize the same returns. **It basically becomes more expensive to prudently invest the older you get.**

You risk not having a recovery period the older you get, so should have less of your assets at risk in volatile investments. You should shift with the Rule of 100 to protect your assets and ensure that they will provide you with the income you need in retirement. Let's look at another example that illustrates how the Rule of 100 becomes more critical as you age. An 80-year-old investor who is retired and is relying on retirement assets for income, for example, needs to depend on a solid amount of Know So Money. The Rule of 100 says an 80-year-old investor should have a maximum of 20 percent of his or her assets at risk. Depending on the investor's financial position, even less risk exposure may be required. You are the only person who can make this kind of determination, but the Rule of 100 can help. Everyone has their own level of comfort. Your Rule of 100 results will be based on your values and attitudes as well as your comfort with risk.

The Rule of 100 can apply to overarching financial management and to specific investment products that you own as well. Take the 401(k) for example. Many people have them, but not many people understand how their money is allocated within their 401(k). An employer may have someone who comes in once a year and explains the models and options that employees can choose from, but that's as much guidance as most 401(k) holders get. Many 401(k) options include target date funds that change their risk exposure over time, essentially following a form of the Rule of 100. Selecting one of these options can often be a good move for employees because they shift your risk as you age, securing more Know So Money when you need it.

A financial professional can look at your assets with you and discuss alternatives to optimize your balance between Know So and Hope So Money.

DEFINING YOUR GOALS

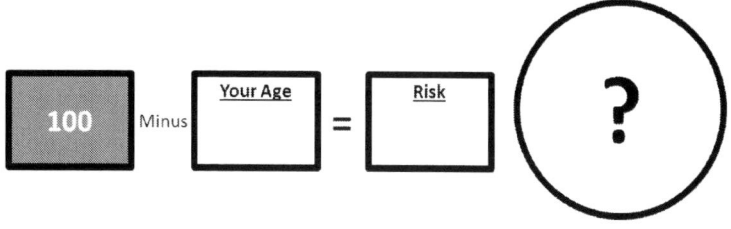

CHAPTER 1 RECAP //

- Start planning for retirement by defining your goals and asking the questions: What do you want your retirement money to do for you? How much money do you need? When do you need that money?
- The rules for retirement planning have changed. Having a planful approach to retirement gives consideration to today's stock market and economy, and the individual concerns of you, the investor.
- Reduce the stress of retirement planning by identifying the difference between the money you hope you'll have and the money you know you'll have. Understanding the difference between the two will help you get back on track to achieving your retirement goals.
- Determining how much risk your assets should be exposed to is achieved through a simple formula known as the "Rule of 100." (100 - [your age] = [percentage of your investments that can comfortably be exposed to risk]) Using this formula gives you a clear picture of the percentage of your assets that should be exposed to risk.

2

THE COLOR OF MONEY

"How much money do I need now, and how much will I need later?"

Richard and Lorraine were nervous about their appointment with their financial professional. Richard was 62 and ready to retire; Lorraine at 58 was still working part-time at her neighborhood church, managing their payroll. Both of them were worried about their retirement nest egg. They knew they had too much of their assets sitting at risk. They experienced some losses during the significant drops in the stock market after 9/11, and then again during the stock market corrections of 2008. They're afraid of another downturn like that happening again during their retirement years and losing 35 to 40 percent of their assets. With the hope of re-growing their money to make up for their losses, they've kept their money where it was, in the stock market. They hope a drop won't happen again, but who really knows what the stock market will do? While it's only logical to assume that a downturn can occur again, they don't know what else they *should be doing, and so they have done nothing, and are feeling a great deal of anxiety about it.*

Securing your accumulated assets so they can provide for you during your retirement begins with an assessment of risk. As identified in the previous chapter, any money that is sitting at risk is considered Hope So Money. In the case of Richard and Lorraine above, their anxiety is directly proportional to the large amount of Hope So Money sitting at risk. If you're planning on protecting and providing for your retirement financially, your next step is to identify how much of your assets are at risk, and then determining the correct proportion of risk necessary for achieving the retirement income you need.

THE STOP LIGHT APPROACH

Over the course of your lifetime, it is likely that you have acquired a variety of assets. Assets can range from money that you have in a savings account or a 401(k), to a pension or an IRA. You have earned money and have made financial decisions based on the best information you had at the time. When viewed as a whole, however, you might not have an overall strategy for the management of your assets. As we have seen, it's more important than ever to know which of your assets are at risk. High market volatility and low treasury rates make for a challenging financial topography. Navigating this financial landscape starts with planful asset management that takes into account your specific needs and options.

In the case of Richard and Lorraine mentioned above, they knew enough to save plenty of money in both their 401(k)s and IRAs, but they didn't know how much risk those investments were exposed to. As a result, they both experienced the pain and anxiety of loss during the market downturn of 2008. During this time, the average investor lost 30 percent of their 401(k) in one year. If more people had shifted their investments away from risk as they neared retirement age – using the Rule of 100 – they might have lost a lot less money going into retirement. Risk is the agent of growth and an important part of any retirement plan. The question is, how much risk is too much risk?

To answer this question, it's useful to assign colors to the different kinds of money according to their risk level. The colors will be familiar to you, because they correspond to the same colors as a traffic light: Red, yellow and green. The same associations that you think of when operating a motor vehicle apply here to managing your retirement money.

Red: This is money currently sitting at risk, in the stock market or in mutual funds. Red money is considered "hope so" money because there is no guarantee it will be there tomorrow. Most red money is considered a liquid asset, meaning it can be cashed in. Just like with a traffic signal, you'll want to stop and think about the safety of these investments as your retirement years approach.

Yellow: This is managed money invested in the stock market, monitored and handled not by a stockbroker but by a certified financial professional. Because it can play a vital role in growing your retirement income, we've dedicated an entire chapter later in the book to "yellow money." This money is usually earmarked for growth and would be considered Red Money if it were not being managed. As the color yellow suggests, someone is keeping an eye on this money daily, increasing the chances that you'll be able to get out or get moving before any significant losses or "accidents" occur.

Green: This is money secured in safer and/or protected accounts with a guaranteed minimum return. Green money is Know So Money because there is little to no risk involved. These types of investments include both liquid and non-liquid investments such as bank CDs, money market accounts, and fixed annuities.

TYPES OF GREEN MONEY: *NEED NOW AND NEED LATER*

Green Money becomes much more important as you age, because this is the money you depend on for income. While you do want to reduce the amount of Red Money and transition a higher percentage of your investments to Green Money, you don't necessarily need all of it to generate income for you right away. Once you have filled the income gap at the beginning of your retirement, you may have money left over. Taking a closer look at Green Money, you will see there are actually different types.

Need Now Green Money is money used for income. As the name suggests, you are relying on this money to provide for your basic needs – pay your bills, purchase your food, and fund recreational activities.

Need Later Green Money is money that you are allowing to accumulate in order to meet your income needs in 5, 10 or 20 years. This is money that you don't need now for income, but you will be relying on down the road. You want to maximize this money by transferring it to a fund where it can earn interest that won't be counted against you. (More about this subject in Chapter 6, "Earning Money by Saving Money.") *Need Later Money* represents income your assets will need to generate for future use. When planning your retirement, it is vital to decide how much of your assets to structure for income and how much to set aside to accumulate to create Need Later Money.

Your Need Now and Need Later Money are top priorities. Creating an income plan ideally allows for both types of green money to be working for you simultaneously. Need Now Money, in particular, will dictate what your options for future needs are.

BALANCING ACT

Determining the amount of risk that is right for you depends on your specific situation. It starts by examining your particular financial position, and determining the percentage of your investments that are considered "at risk." When using the Rule of 100 to calculate your level of risk, your financial age might be different than your chronological age.

The way you balance the risk associated with your assets depends on your individual goals and your level of comfort with risk. In Richard and Lorraine's case, it made sense to portion 35 percent of their investments as red money and 65 percent as green. We looked at index annuities for the green section, and a managed portfolio for the 35 percent in red. A managed portfolio is considered yellow money. It gives a better rate of return than green money, but with less risk than red money. In their case, it was possible to have less risk in the 35 percent earmarked for red by placing the money in a managed portfolio. In the end, they had a higher return than they had when 80 percent of their investments were in the red. That coupled with the percent of their investments in green money took all the stress out of their retirement planning. The tension left their faces, and they left the meeting knowing they could do this, because now, they had a "know so" plan in place.

Whatever you determine the appropriate amount of risk to be, you will need to organize your portfolio to reflect your goals. If you have more Red Money than Green Money, in particular, you will need to make decisions about how to move it. Working with a financial professional is one way to find appropriate Green and Yellow Money options for your situation.

Investing heavily in Red Money and gambling all of your assets on the market is incredibly risky no matter where you fall within the Rule of 100. Money in the market can't be depended on to generate income, and a plan that leans too heavily on Red Money can easily fail, especially when investment decisions are influenced by emotional reactions to market downturns and recoveries. Not only is this an unwise plan, it can be incredibly stressful to an investor who is gambling everything on stocks and mutual funds.

But a plan that uses too much Green Money avoids all volatility and can also fail. Why? Investing all of your money in Certificates of Deposit (CDs), savings accounts, money markets and other low return accounts may provide interest and income, but that likely won't be enough to keep pace with inflation. If you focus exclusively on income from Green Money and avoid owning any stocks or mutual funds in your portfolio, you won't be able to leverage the potential for long-term growth your portfolio needs to stay healthy and productive. This is where the Rule of 100 can help you determine how much of your money should be invested in the market to anticipate your future needs.

THE NUMBERS DON'T LIE

When the rubber meets the road, the numbers dictate your options. Your risk tolerance is an important indicator of what kinds of investments you should consider, but if the returns from those investments don't meet your retirement goals, your income needs will likely not be met.

For example, if the level of risk you are comfortable with manages your investments at a 4 percent return and you need to realize an 8 percent return, your income needs aren't going to be met when you need to rely on your investments for retirement income. A professional may encourage you to be more aggressive with your investment strategy by taking on more risk in order to give you the potential of earning a greater return. If taking more risk isn't an option that you are comfortable with, then the discussion will turn to how you can earn more money or spend less in order to align your needs with your resources more closely.

How are you going to structure your income flow during retirement? The answer to this question dictates how you determine your risk tolerance. If the numbers say that you need to be more aggressive with your investing, or that you need to modify your lifestyle, it becomes a choice you need to make.

BEYOND THE NUMBERS

While the Rule of 100 is a useful way to begin to deliberate the right amount of risk for you, it is just a baseline. Use it as a starting point for figuring out where your money should be. If you're a 50-year-old investor, the Rule of 100 suggests that you have 50 percent Green Money and 50 percent Red Money. Most 50-year-olds are more risk tolerant, however. There are many reasons why someone might be more risk tolerant, not the least of which is feeling young! Experienced investors, people who feel they need to gamble for a higher return, or people who have met their retirement income goals and are looking for additional ways to accumulate wealth are all candidates for investment strategies that incorporate higher levels of risk. In the end, it comes down to your personal tolerance for risk. How much are you willing to lose?

Consulting with a financial professional is often the wisest approach to calculating your risk level. A professional can help determine your risk tolerance by getting to know you, asking you a set of questions and even giving you a survey to determine your comfort level with different types of risk. Here's a typical scenario a financial professional might pose to you:

"You have $100,000 saved that you would like to invest in the market. There is an investment product that could turn your $100,000 into $120,000. That same option, however, has the potential of losing you up to $30,000, leaving you with $70,000."

Is that a scenario that you are willing to enter into? Or are you more comfortable with this one:

"You could turn your $100,000 into $110,000, but have the potential of losing $15,000, leaving you with $85,000."

Your answer to these and others types of questions will help a financial professional determine what level of risk is right for you. They can then offer you investment strategies and management plans that reflect your financial age, and not just your age in years. Organizing your assets, understanding the color of your money, and creating an income and accumulation plan for retirement can quickly become an overwhelming task. The fact of the matter is that financial professionals build their careers around understanding the different variables affecting retirement financing. You might have a million dollars socked away in a savings account, but your neighbor, who has $300,000 in a diverse investment portfolio that is tailored to their needs, may end up enjoying a better retirement lifestyle. Why? Because they had a planful approach.

CHAPTER 2 RECAP //
- Your investment portfolio can be looked at in terms of colors, using the same signals as on a traffic light. Red Money represents money at risk; Yellow Money is managed money and has less risk than red but more risk than green, and Green Money is safer money, with little to no exposure to risk.
- There are two types of Green Money: Need Now and Need Later. It is important to structure your investments to provide you with income for both now and later.
- Working with a Registered Investment Advisor will help you compose a clear and concise picture of the risk assigned to your assets to help you manage them in a balanced way.

3
CREATING AN INCOME PLAN
"Are you ready for The Cliff?"

Dan and Carol had children later in life, and paying for their college education was one of their most pressing concerns when planning for retirement. Because this was an important goal for them, they met with a financial planner to see if this was possible. After looking at the numbers, they streamlined their monthly needs and postponed travel plans. They calculated they could get by comfortably and pay for their daughter's medical school and their son's four-year college with a monthly budget of $5,000 during the first 8 years of their retirement. They each had a small pension coming in for a monthly total of $1,500 and their combined Social Security benefits would give them another $2,500. But this created a $1,000 a month gap or shortage in their desired goal. They did have a $250,000 IRA that was earning 5 percent interest, and so they decided to supplement their monthly income shortage by drawing $1,000 month out of the IRA. They did this for several years. Fortunately, they were able to sustain the value of their IRA by having it in a guaranteed account earning 5 percent interest, at $12,500 a year. This amounted to $500 more per year than they were taking out. The IRA was in an indexed annuity, so it never lost money, sustained itself and even grew a little bit.

Ten years down the road, after their children had both graduated debt-free, Carol's mother died. Carol inherited another $250,000, after taxes. Dan and Carol were able to stop drawing off the IRA – which is fully taxable when withdrawn – and take that same $1,000 a month from the inheritance, which was tax free money. That saved them several thousand dollars a year in income taxes, yet kept their income and their lifestyle exactly the same. It also meant they could finally take that trip to Iceland they had always dreamed of.

Because circumstances often arise, the best income plans allow for flexibility and change. Using the goals you identified in Chapter One, creating an income plan begins with an evaluation of your daily income needs. Finding the most efficient and beneficial way to address them will have impacts on your lifestyle, your asset accumulation and your legacy planning after you retire. When you have identified your goals and income needs, you will know how much to structure for income and how much to be set aside for accumulation.

Every financial strategy for retirement needs first to accommodate the day-to-day need for income. The moment your working income ceases and you start living off the money you've set aside for retirement is referred to as the **retirement cliff**. When you begin drawing income from your retirement assets, you have entered the distribution phase of your financial plan. *The distribution phase of your retirement plan* is when you reach the point of relying on your assets for income. This is where your Green Money comes into play: the safer, more reliable assets that you have accumulated that are designed to provide you with a steady income. On day one of your retirement, you will need a steady and reliable supply of income from your Green Money.

TURNING ON THE STREAMS

The most common sources of income during retirement are pensions, Social Security benefits, and accumulated money set up in traditional or ROTH IRAs. Identify the source and the amount of the income, as well as its frequency.

Next, determine when those streams need to be turned on, and how long they need to run. Ask yourself, when do you need the money? And how long do you need the money for? The best plans are those that aren't cast in stone. They allow for some flexibility. If there is an inheritance that may come into effect somewhere down the road, or if the death of a spouse occurs, your income needs will change. Slowing down or switching off those income streams should be options built into your plan so it can be adjusted to life's changing needs.

UTILIZING THE LEAST AMOUNT OF ACCUMULATION FOR THE MOST GROWTH

When your income streams fall short of your actual income needs, things start to get interesting. This is where it becomes even more vital to the health of your retirement income stream to seek counsel from a financial professional. We can take a look at your other assets and create or revise an income plan using those other assets earmarked for retirement in the most effective way possible. ***Our goal is to use the LEAST amount of your other assets to generate the income you need to fill that gap.*** We want to keep as much of your assets as we can in growth mode, because the more the assets, the more the potential growth. This is our rule of thumb, and it can provide a guideline for you as well when deciding how to best position your other assets to fill your income gap.

Understanding your Social Security benefit, filling the income gap and making an overall plan that meets your retirement income needs is no small task. Once you have worked with a financial professional to structure your income needs, it's time to take a look at the future. *With your immediate income needs met, you have the opportunity to take your additional assets and leverage them for profit to supplement your income in the future, to prepare for anticipated health care costs or to contribute to your legacy.* Stable income also means that you should have the staying power to stick with your investment portfolio through the ups and downs in the market.

MATH OF REBOUNDS

A fickle market can raise the eyebrows of even the most veteran investor. Taking a hit in the market hurts no matter how stable your income. Part of the pain comes from knowing that when you take a step back in the market, it requires an even larger step forward to return to where you were. For example, if you have a red money account that loses 50 percent of its value due to a stock market drop, it doesn't just take a 50 percent gain to get your account back to even. *It requires a 100 percent gain just to get you back to where you were before.* In today's market, that type of return would be very challenging to achieve over a period of years, because the chances are pretty good you may suffer yet another decline. The math of rebounds dictates that the percentage of loss does not equal the percentage of the gain required to break even again. A loss of 10 percent requires an 11 percent gain. A 25 percent loss requires a 33 percent gain to get back to even. However the mathematical formula works out, it always takes several years to get back to even, and remember, you aren't earning any interest or gaining at all during those years. That's why in a number of cases, the hybrid approach using an indexed annuity (to be discussed in Chapter 5) makes so much sense, because you're eliminating any and all risk of stock market drops.

CHAPTER 3 RECAP //
- Creating an income plan begins with identifying your monthly income needs, your income streams, and then filling in the gaps.
- The best income plans are flexible and able to handle the changing circumstances of life.
- Determine the LEAST amount of assets required for the MOST amount of growth when determining which assets to utilize when filling gaps in your income.
- The math of rebounds dictates that the percentage of money lost does not equal the percentage of money required to break even again.

4
UNDERSTANDING SOCIAL SECURITY

"When should I start taking my Social Security benefits?"

One kind of Green Money that most Americans can rely on for income when they retire is Social Security. If you're like most Americans, Social Security is or will be an important part of your retirement income and one that you should know how to properly manage.

As a first step in creating your income plan, a financial professional will take a look at your Social Security benefit options. Social Security is the foundation of income planning for anyone who is about to retire and is a reliable source of Green Money in your overall income plan. But there is no one-size-fits-all answer to the question of "When should I take my Social Security benefit?" Everybody's health and situations are different.

> » *Irene was a dental assistant who retired at age 62. She immediately started taking her Social Security benefit without*

really thinking about it, and the payments started coming in the mail. One day when Irene was getting the mail, the subject of Social Security came up during a conversation with one of her friends. This friend confided to Irene that she was waiting to take her Social Security benefits, because doing so would mean $800 more per month in income! Irene couldn't believe it. Had she waited just four more years, her annual income could have gone up by $9,600 dollars. But there wasn't anything she could do about this mistake now, because she had been taking her benefits for more than year.

» *At the other end of the Social Security question we have Abby, a retired real estate agent who decided to wait until she was 70 to draw her Social Security benefits. She knew age 70 was when she could get the maximum amount of benefit, and so Abby waited even though she retired at age 62. On the day before her 67th birthday, Abby was diagnosed with pancreatic cancer. It had already spread into her lungs and at that point, Abby knew her condition was fatal. She lasted another 6 months before passing away without ever taking so much as $1 of the benefit she'd worked all her life to earn. She wasn't able to pass on any of this money to her beneficiaries, either. Had she started at 62, she could at least have gotten 5 full years of payment. As it was, the government kept all her money.*

Here are some facts that illustrate how Americans currently use Social Security:

- 90 percent of Americans age 65 and older receive Social Security benefits.*
- Social Security provides 39 percent of income for retired Americans.*

---

*http://www.ssa.gov/pressoffice/basicfact.htm

- Claiming Social Security benefits at the wrong time can reduce your monthly benefit by up to 57 percent.**
- 43 percent of men and 48 percent of women claim Social Security benefits at age 62.**
- 74 percent of retirees receive reduced Social Security benefits.**
- In 2013, the average monthly Social Security benefit was $1,261. *The maximum benefit for 2013 was $2,533. The $1,272 monthly benefit reduction between the average and the maximum is applied for life.****

There are many aspects of Social Security that are well known and others that aren't. When it comes time for you to cash in on your Social Security benefit, you will have many options and choices. Social Security is a massive government program that manages retirement benefits for millions of people. Experts spend their entire careers understanding and analyzing it. Luckily, you don't have to understand all of the intricacies of Social Security to maximize its advantages. You simply need to know the best way to manage your Social Security benefit. You need to know exactly what to do to get the most from your Social Security benefit and when to do it. Taking the time to create a roadmap for your Social Security strategy will help ensure that you are able to exact your maximum benefit and efficiently coordinate it with the rest of your retirement plan.

There are many aspects of Social Security that you have no control over. You don't control how much you put into it, and you don't control what it's invested in or how the government manages it. However, you do control when and how you file for benefits. The real question about Social Security that you need to answer is, "When should I start taking Social Security?" While

---

**When to Claim Social Security Benefits, David Blanchett, CFA, CFP® January, 2013
***http://www.socialsecurity.gov/pressoffice/factsheets/colafacts2013.com

this is the all-important question, there are a couple of key pieces of information you need to track down first.

Before we get into a few calculations and strategies that can make all the difference, let's start by covering the basic information about Social Security which should give you an idea of where you stand. Just as the foundation of a house creates the stable platform for the rest of the framework to rest upon, your Social Security benefit is an important part of your overall retirement plan. The purpose of the information that follows is not to give an exhaustive explanation of how Social Security works, but to give you some tools and questions to start understanding how Social Security affects your retirement and how you can prepare for it. Let's start with eligibility.

Eligibility. Understanding how and when you are eligible for Social Security benefits will help clarify what to expect when the time comes to claim them.

To receive retirement benefits from Social Security, you must earn eligibility. In almost all cases, Americans born after 1929 must earn 40 quarters of credit to be eligible to draw their Social Security retirement benefit. In 2013, a Social Security credit represents $1,160 earned in a calendar quarter. The number changes as it is indexed each year, but not drastically. In 2012, a credit represented $1,130. Four quarters of credit is the maximum number that can be earned each year. In 2013, an American would have had to earn at least $4,640 to accumulate four credits. In order to qualify for retirement benefits, you must earn a minimum number of credits. Additionally, if you are at least 62 years old and have been married to a recipient of Social Security benefits for at least 12 months, you can choose to receive Spousal Benefits. Although 40 is the minimum number of credits required to begin drawing benefits, it is important to know that once you claim your Social Security benefit, there is no going back. Although there may be cost of living adjustments made, you are locked into that base benefit amount forever.

Primary Insurance Amount. You can think of your Primary Insurance Amount (PIA) like a ripening fruit. It represents the amount of your Social Security benefit at your Full Retirement Age (FRA). If you opt to take benefits before your FRA, however, your monthly benefit will be less than your PIA. You will essentially be picking an unripened fruit. On the one hand, waiting until after your FRA to access your benefits will increase your benefit beyond your PIA. On the other hand, you don't want the fruit to overripen, because every month you wait is one less check you get from the government.

Full Retirement Age. Your FRA is an important number for anyone who is planning to rely on Social Security benefits in their retirement. Depending on when you were born, there is a specific age at which you will attain FRA. Your FRA is dictated by your year of birth and is the age at which you can begin your full monthly benefit. Your FRA is important because it is half of the equation used to calculate your Social Security benefit. The other half of the equation is based on when you start taking benefits.

When Social Security was initially set up, the FRA was age 65, and it still is for people born before 1938. But as time has passed, the age for receiving full retirement benefits has increased. If you were born between 1938 and 1960, your full retirement age is somewhere on a sliding scale between 65 and 67. Anyone born in 1960 or later will now have to wait until age 67 for full benefits. Increasing the FRA has helped the government reduce the cost of the Social Security program, which pays out more than a half trillion dollars to beneficiaries every year!*

While you can begin collecting benefits as early as age 62, the amount you receive as a monthly benefit will be less than it would be if you wait until you reached or surpassed your FRA. It is im-

---

A Social Security Owner's Manual, Blankenship, 2013

portant to note that if you file for Social Security benefit before your FRA, *the reduction to your monthly benefit will remain in place for the rest of your life.* You can also delay receiving benefits up to age 70, in which case your benefits will be higher than your PIA for the rest of your life.

- At FRA, 100 percent of PIA is available as a monthly benefit.
- At age 62, your Social Security retirement benefits are available. For each month you take benefits prior to your FRA, however, the monthly amount of your benefit is reduced. *This reduction stays in place for the rest of your life.*
- At age 70, your monthly benefit reaches its maximum. After you turn age 70, your monthly benefit will no longer increase.

Year of birth	Full Retirement Age
1943-1954	66
1955	66 and 2 months
1956	66 and 4 months
1957	66 and 6 months
1958	66 and 8 months
1959	66 and 10 months
1960 or later	67*

ROLLING UP YOUR SOCIAL SECURITY

Your Social Security income "rolls up" the longer you wait to claim it. Your monthly benefit will continue to increase until you turn 70 years old. But because Social Security is the foundation of most people's retirement, many Americans feel that they don't have control over how or when they receive their benefits. As a matter of fact, only 4 percent of Americans wait until after their

*Social Security Administration

FRA to file for benefits! This trend persists, despite the fact that every dollar you increase your Social Security income by means less money you will have to spend from your nest egg to meet your retirement income needs! For many people, creating their Social Security strategy is the most important decision they can make to positively impact their retirement. ***The difference between the best and worst Social Security decision can be tens of thousands of dollars over a lifetime of benefits — up to $170,000!***

Deciding NOW or LATER: Following the above logic, it makes sense to wait as long as you can to begin receiving your Social Security benefit. However, the answer isn't always that simple. Not everyone has the option of waiting. Many people need to rely on Social Security on day one of their retirement. In fact, **nearly 50 percent of 62-year-old Americans file for Social Security benefits**. Why is this number so high? Some might need the income. Others might be in poor health and don't feel they will live long enough to make FRA worthwhile for themselves or their families. It is also possible, however, that the majority of folks taking an early benefit at age 62 are simply under-informed about Social Security. Perhaps they make this major decision based on rumors and emotion.

File Immediately if You:
- Find your job is unbearable.
- Are willing to sacrifice retirement income.
- Are not healthy and need a reliable source of income.

Consider Delaying Your Benefit if You:
- Want to maximize your retirement income.
- Want to increase retirement benefits for your spouse.
- Are still working and like it.
- Are healthy and willing / able to wait to file.

So if you decide to wait, how long should you wait? Lots of people can put it off for a few years, but not everyone can wait until they are 70 years old. Your individual circumstances may be able to help you determine when you should begin taking Social Security. If you do the math, you will quickly see that between ages 62 and 70, there are 96 months in which you can file for your Social Security benefit. If you take into account those 96 months and the 96 months your spouse could also file for Social Security, the number of different strategies for structuring your benefit, you can easily end up with more than 20,000 different scenarios. It's safe to say this isn't the kind of math that most people can easily handle. Each month would result in a different benefit amount. The longer you wait, the higher your monthly benefit amount becomes. Each month you wait, however, is one less month that you receive a Social Security check.

The goal is to maximize your lifetime benefits. That may not always mean waiting until you can get the largest monthly payment. Taking the bigger picture into account, you want to find out how to get the most money out of Social Security over the number of years that you draw from it. Don't underestimate the power of optimizing your benefit: the difference between the BEST and WORST Social Security election can easily be between $30,000 to $50,000 in lifetime benefits.

The difference can be very substantial!

It might help to use an analogy of ripening fruit. Every year that you wait to collect Social Security, your benefit grows, getting fatter and plumper each year. The trick here is to pick the fruit of your benefit at its peak, before it goes bad. If you don't take your benefits the first year that it can start, at age 62, and you wait, those benefits will continue to ripen at a rate of about 6 percent per year until age 66. Between ages 66 to 70, the fruit ripens even faster, and the benefit gets bigger, rolling up to 8 percent per year. After age 70, the fruit stops growing. Like an apple that has dropped from the tree, there is never a point after age 70 where the fruit can get any bigger. So you know you want to pick the fruit at its peak ripeness, but how do you determine what that means for you?

Financial professionals have access to software that will calculate the best year and month for you to file for benefits based on your default life expectancy. You can further customize that information by estimating your life expectancy based on your health, habits and family history. If you can then create an income plan (we'll get into this later in the chapter) that helps you wait until the target date for you to file for Social Security, you can optimize your retirement income strategy to get the most out of your Social Security benefit. How can you calculate your life expectancy? Well, you don't know exactly how long you'll live, but you have a better idea than the government does. They rely on averages to make their calculations. ***You have much more personal information about your health, lifestyle and family history than they do.*** You can use that knowledge to game the system and beat all the other people who are making uninformed decisions by filing early for Social Security.

While you can and should educate yourself about how Social Security works, the reality is you don't need to know a lot of general information about Social Security in order to make choices about your retirement. What you do need to know is exactly **what to do to maximize your benefit.** For most Americans, Social Security is the foundation of income planning for retirement. Social Security benefits represent nearly 40 percent of the income of retirees.* For many people, it can represent the largest portion of their retirement income. Not treating your Social Security benefit as an asset and investment tool can lead to sub-optimization of one of your largest sources of retirement income.

---

*http://www.socialsecurity.gov/pressoffice/basicfact.htm

Let's take a look at an example that shows the impact of working with a financial professional to optimize Social Security benefits:

> » *Peter and Martha Ooley are a typical American couple who have worked their whole lives and saved when they could. Peter is 60 years old, and Martha is 56 years old. They sat down with a financial professional who logged onto the Social Security website to look up their PIAs. Peter's PIA is $1,900 and Martha's is $900.*
>
> *If the Ooleys cash in at age 62 and begin taking retirement benefits from Social Security, they will receive an estimated $492,000 in lifetime benefits. That may seem like a lot, but if you divide that amount over 20 years, it averages out to be just shy of $25,000 per year. The Ooleys are accustomed to a more significant annual income than that. To make up the difference, they will have to rely on alternative retirement income options. They will basically have to depend on a bigger nest egg to provide them with the income they need.*
>
> *If they wait until their FRA, they will increase their lifetime benefits to an estimated $523,700. This option allows them to achieve their Primary Insurance Amount, which will provide them a $33,000 annual income.*
>
> *After learning the Ooleys' needs and using software to calculate the most optimal time to begin drawing benefits, their financial professional determined that the best option for them drastically increases their potential lifetime benefits to $660,000!*
>
> *By using strategies that their financial professional recommended, Pete and Martha increased their potential lifetime benefits by as much as **$148,000**. There's no telling how much you could miss out on from your Social Security if you don't take time to create a strategy that calculates your maximum benefit. For the Ooleys, the value of maximizing their benefits*

was the difference between night and day. While this may seem like a special case, it isn't uncommon to find benefit increases of this magnitude. You'll never know unless you take a look at your own options.

Despite the importance of knowing when and how to take your Social Security benefit, many of today's retirees and pre-retirees may know little about the mechanics of Social Security and how they can maximize their benefit.

So, to whom should you turn for advice when making this complex decision? Before you pick up the phone and call Uncle Sam, you should know that the Social Security Administration (SSA) representatives are actually prohibited from giving you election advice! Plus, SSA representatives in general are trained to focus on monthly benefit amounts, not the lifetime income for a family.

MAXIMIZING YOUR LIFETIME BENEFIT

As discussed in Chapter 2, calculating how to maximize **lifetime benefits** is more important than waiting until age 70 for your maximum **monthly benefit amount**. It's about getting the most income during your lifetime. **There's really no way a person can determine when to take Social Security unless they understand all the different options that are available to them.** Professional benefit-maximization software can target the year and month that it is most beneficial for you to file based on your life expectancy.

The three most common ages that people associate with retirement benefits are 62 (Earliest Eligible Age), 66 (Full Retirement Age), and 70 (age at which monthly maximum benefit is reached). In almost all circumstances, however, none of those three most common ages will give you the maximum lifetime benefit.

Remember, every month you wait to file, the amount of your benefit check goes up, but you also get one less check. You don't know how exactly how long you're going to live, but you have a better idea of your life expectancy than the actuaries at the Social Security Administration who can only work with averages. They can't make calculations based on your specific situation. A professional can run the numbers for you and get the target date that maximizes your potential lifetime benefits. You can't get this information from the SSA, but you *can* get it from a financial professional.

Your Social Security options don't stop here, however. There are a plethora of other choices you can make to manipulate your benefit payments.

Just a Few Types of Social Security Benefits:
- Retired Worker Benefit. This is the benefit with which most people are familiar. The Retired Worker Benefit is what most people are talking about when they refer to Social Security. It is your benefit based on your earnings and the amount that you have paid into the system over the span of your career.
- Spousal Benefit. The Spousal Benefit is available to the spouse of someone who is eligible for Retired Worker Benefits. What if there was a way for your spouse to receive his or her benefit for four years and not lose the chance to get his or her maximum benefit when he or she turns age 70? Many people do not know about this strategy and might be missing out on benefits they have earned.
- Survivorship Benefit. When one spouse passes away, the survivor is able to receive the larger of the two benefit amounts.
- File and Suspend. This concept allows for a lower-earning spouse to receive up to 50 percent of the other's PIA amount if both spouses file for benefits at the right time.

- Restricted Application. A higher-earning spouse may be able to start collecting a spousal benefit on the lower-earning spouse's benefit while allowing his or her benefit to continue to grow.

THE DIVORCE FACTOR

How does a divorced spouse qualify for benefits? If you have gone through a divorce, it might affect the retirement benefit to which you are entitled.

A person can receive benefits as a divorced spouse on a former spouse's Social Security record if he or she:
- Was married to the former spouse for at least 10 years;
- Is at least age 62 years old;
- Is unmarried; and
- Is not entitled to a higher Social Security benefit on his or her own record.*

With all of the different options, strategies and benefits to choose from, you can see why filing for Social Security is more complicated than just mailing in the paperwork. Gathering the data and making yourself aware of all your different options isn't enough to know exactly what to do, however. On the one hand, you can knock yourself out trying to figure out which options are best for you and wondering if you made the best decision. On the other hand, you can work with a financial professional who uses customized software that takes all the variables of your specific situation into account and calculates your best option. You have tens of thousands of different options for filing for your Social Security benefit. If your spouse is a different age than you are, it nearly doubles the amount of options you have. This is far more complicated arithmetic than most people can do on their own. If you want a truly accurate understanding of when and how to file, you need someone who will ask you the right questions about

---

*http://www.ssa.gov/retire2/yourdivspouse.htm

your situation, someone who has access to specialized software that can crunch the numbers. The reality is that you need to work with a professional that can provide you with the sophisticated analysis of your situation that will help you make a truly informed decision.

Important Questions about Your Social Security Benefit:
- How can I maximize my lifetime benefit? By knowing when and how to file for Social Security. This usually means waiting until you have at least reached your Full Retirement Age. A professional has the experience and the tools to help determine when and how you can maximize your lifetime benefits.
- Who will provide reliable advice for making these decisions? Only a professional has the tools and experience to provide you reliable advice.
- Will the Social Security Administration provide me with the advice? The Social Security Administration cannot provide you with advice or strategies for claiming your benefit. They can give you information about your monthly benefit, but that's it. They also don't have the tools to tell you what your specific best option is. They can accurately answer how the system works, but they can't advise you on what decision to make as to how and when to file for benefits.
- Can I change my mind after I start taking my Social Security benefits? Few people are aware of the grace period granted by the Federal Government when it comes to taking your Social Security benefits. **A person can change their Social Security election as long as they do these two things: change it within the first 12 months of electing it, and pay back all of the benefits received.** For example, if you're age 62 ½, you would need to make

the change before you reach age 63 ½. Additionally, you would have to pay back all of the benefits received during that first year.

The Maximization Report that your financial professional will generate represents an invaluable resource for understanding how and when to file for your Social Security benefit. When you get your customized Social Security Maximization Report, you will not only know all the options available to you – but you will understand the financial implications of each choice. In addition to the analysis, you will also get a report that shows exactly at what age – including which month and year – you should trigger benefits and how you should apply. It also includes a variety of other time-specific recommendations, such as when to apply for Medicare or take Required Minimum Distributions from your qualified plans. A report means there is no need to wonder, or to try to figure out when to take action – the Social Security Maximization Report lays it all out for you in plain English.

CHAPTER 4 RECAP //

- An Investment Advisor can help you determine when you should file for Social Security to get your Maximum Lifetime Benefit.
- To get the most out of your Social Security benefit, you need to file at the right time.
- If you change your mind about when you wish to receive your Social Security benefit, you have the option to cancel as long as you do it within the first year of receiving benefits and pay back the full dollar amount of all benefits received.
- Integrating your Social Security options with the rest of your income plan will give you an idea of how much more money you need.

- Every dollar your Social Security income increases is less money you'll have to spend from your nest egg to supplement your income.
- After Social Security and your additional income are accounted for, the amount that's left to meet your needs is called the Income Gap.

5
MYTHS AND REALITIES OF ANNUITIES

"Will Social Security be enough?"

You've worked and earned money your whole life, but the day that you retire, that income comes to an end. That's the day you start turning on those other income streams, and relying on your benefits such as Social Security. For many people approaching the retirement cliff, those income streams simply aren't enough. This shortfall is called the **Income Gap** and it needs to be filled in order to maintain your lifestyle into retirement. You also want to know how to fill that income gap with the fewest dollars possible, because you need the muscle of accumulation to help your retirement nest keep up with the cost of inflation. One investment tool that can help you accomplish both of these goals with little or no risk to your capital is something known as an annuity.

THE BAD APPLE OF INVESTMENTS

Annuities have gotten such a bad reputations over the years, many people have decided not to have anything to do with them at all. This is a little akin to watching someone discover a worm in their apple, and then deciding that from then on out, you will never eat another apple again. While it's true that bad apples and bad annuities do exist, the converse of that statement is also true. If you've been shying away from annuities, then you've been missing out on a largely safe, "know so" green-money way to grow your retirement assets.

To help explain what an annuity is, let's shed some light on what they are not by covering a few of the myths you might have heard about annuities. While annuities have been around since the 1980s, these myths came about a few years ago. Several lawsuits happened after a handful of unscrupulous advisors who were not even financial professionals didn't share with their clients the structure of surrender fees and other charges associated with their annuities. There was a lot of bad press and media all over the internet, during which time annuities were put under a lot of negative scrutiny. To help set the facts straight, let's pull back the curtain on a few of the more popular urban legends and shed some light onto what annuities are actually designed to do.

Myth #1: You can't ever get all your money out of the annuity. The reason this myth started is due to one kind of annuity still available today known as an immediate annuity with a life income option. If you put your money in an immediate annuity, it means what its name suggests: the annuity starts paying immediately. This might be desirable if you have a lump sum of money that you'd like to turn into an income stream. If you elect the "life income option" for that immediate annuity, then you can't get your principal back. In other words, you can't get your money out of the annuity. In exchange, you get an income stream that is guaranteed for the rest of your life. Very few people use this "life income" option now.

Reality #1: You can get all of your money out of the annuity after the surrender charge period unless you have purchased *an immediate annuity with a life income option.* This is a very specific kind of annuity and many investment companies no longer even offer this as an option.

Myth #2: All annuities are bad. Not all annuities are Green Money options. There are some annuities that rely on the stock market and are actually considered a Red Money option. These are known as variable annuities and they could be part of your Red Money portfolio. If you're interested in a variable annuity, make sure you ask your financial professional about any fees and surrender charges.

Reality #2: Annuities are a useful investing tool designed to provide a good source of income during retirement. Annuities pay out a set income that never goes down, and in some cases can go even go up. At the same time, annuities can form part of your legacy, providing money for your beneficiaries without the expense and delay of probate. Some annuities are linked to the stock market, but they don't come with the volatile up and down swings. You can't get any of those high returns, but you also can't lose any of the principal. We recommend them as a green money option not to be compared to the stock market, but to be considered similar to a bank CD.

Myth #3: The surrender fees or early withdrawal charges are so high, it's not worth it. Some annuities do have pretty significant surrender charges, but there are several insurance companies that offer annuities with no surrender fees or early withdrawal charges. They do exist, so ask for them.

Reality #3: *Most annuities carry a provision that allows for a 10 percent free annual withdrawal based on your entire balance.* This means that if you have a $250,000 annuity, you can withdraw up to $25,000 annually without penalty. You could literally get all of it this way, withdrawing it over 12 years, taking out 10 percent each year, in which case you would receive a much higher rate of interest than you would on a bank account during that same period of time.

In general, annuities aren't recommended for anything short of a long term investment timeframe. The ones that come with the longest terms of surrender and the highest percentage penalty typically pay the highest rate of interest to your annuity, so you have control over what you decide. Shorter terms with smaller penalties also exist, and they generally pay lower rates. Once an annuity is mature, (meaning the surrender charge has been eliminated) you can take the lump sum and move it, or do anything else with it you like without any penalty. You can also leave it intact, or roll it into a new annuity with potentially more features. With an annuity that's been renewed (i.e. continued on "as is"), there will never be any further early withdrawal charges because it is past the surrender charge period.

Myth #4: Annuities are too complex to understand, therefore, I shouldn't have one. While by and large you don't want to make an investment you don't understand, the focus needs to remain on the concept of what an indexed annuity can do for you rather than the intricate details and complexities of how they arrive at the interest rate that credits to your annuity account. To understand the basic premise, make sure that your advisor spends sufficient time explaining how the annuity works.

Reality #4: Focus on the concept of what the annuity can do for you rather than how it does it. As a green money asset, if you can get a 6 or 8 percent interest rate with a guarantee of your

principal, the formulas used to arrive at how that interest accrues becomes less important. Here is what annuities can offer you:
- Tax deferred growth
- Stock market linked interest
- Higher income payout
- Greater safety of principal
- Avoidance of probate through use of a designated beneficiary
- Can be used for an IRA or non-qualified money

TAKING A HYBRID APPROACH TO YOUR INCOME NEEDS

If you are concerned about the best way to fill your income gap, an income annuity investment tool is likely a good option for you. Income annuities have many similar qualities to Social Security that give them the same look and feel as that reliable benefit check you get every month. The difference is, with annuities, you have the option of putting more money into them in order to get more out. They also have the potential to increase the value of your principal investment.

It's not about whether the market goes up or down, but when it does. If you are directly invested in the market and it goes down at the wrong time for your five or ten year retirement horizon, you could be in serious danger of losing some of your retirement income. If you have assets that you would like to structure for retirement income, **an annuity may be the right choice for you.**

Ask yourself the following questions:
- How concerned are you about finding a secure financial vehicle to protect your savings?
- How concerned are you that there may be a better way to structure your savings?

HOW ANNUITIES FIT INTO AN OVERALL INCOME PLAN

In its simplest form, an annuity is a way to invest your money that allows you to structure it for income. Annuities come in a variety of modes with various features. Finding the right one for you will take a conversation with your financial professional.

While it's not necessary to understand the inner workings of how an annuity arrives at its calculations, be sure you do understand its benefits, features, and cost to you before investing your money.

For those who are interested, what follows is a description of the inner-working of the annuity world:

When you put your money into an annuity, you are essentially buying an investment product from an insurance company. It is a contract between you and the insurance company that provides the investment vehicle. Let's say you have saved $100,000 and need it to generate income to meet your needs above and beyond your Social Security and pension checks. You give the $100,000 to an insurance company, who in turn invests it to generate growth.

They usually select investments that have modest returns over long term horizons. In other words, they generally put it somewhere stable and predictable. Most commonly, they will invest it in a combination of bonds and treasuries that are safer and dependable ways to grow money. They use the money from the insurance products they sell to invest, use a portion of the returns to generate profits for themselves, and return a portion to clients in the form of payouts, claims, and structured income options.

One of the most attractive qualities of these types of annuities is something called *annual reset*. **Annual reset** is sometimes also referred to as a "ratcheting." Instead of taking on the risk that comes with putting money in a fluctuating market, you can offset that risk onto the insurance company. It works like this: If the market goes down, you don't suffer a loss. Instead, the insurance company absorbs it. But if the market goes up, you share with the insurance company some of the profit made on the gain. The amount of gain you get is called your annuity participation rate. Typically the insurer will cap the amount of gain you can realize at somewhere between 3 and 7 percent. If the market goes up 10 percent, you would realize a portion of that gain (whatever percentage you are capped at). This means you to never lose money on your investment, while always gaining a portion of the upswings. The measurement period of your annuity can be calculated monthly, weekly and even daily, but most annuities are measured annually. The level of the index when you buy and the index level one year later will generally determine the amount of loss or gain. You and the insurance company are betting that the market will generally go up over time.

INCOME RIDER

When you use that $100,000 to buy a contract with an insurance company in the form of an annuity, you are pegging your money on an index. It could be the S&P 500, the Dow Jones Industrial Average or any number of other indexes. To generate income from the annuity, you select something called an income rider. An income rider is an option of an indexed annuity. Essentially, it is the amount of money from which the insurance company will pay you an income while you have your money in their annuity. Your income rider is a larger number than what your investment is actually worth, and if you select the income rider, it will increase in value over time, providing you with more income. As the insurance company holds your money and invests it, they generate a return on it that they use to pay you a regular monthly income based on a higher number. The insurance company has to outperform the amount that they pay you in order to make a profit.

Remember, insurance companies make long-term investments that provide them with predictable flows of money. They like to stabilize the amount of money that goes in and out of their doors instead of paying and receiving large unpredictable chunks at once. When you opt for an income rider, an insurance company can reliably predict how much money they will pay out to you over a set period of time. It's predictable, and they like that. They can base their business on those predictable numbers.

This is a hypothetical illustration

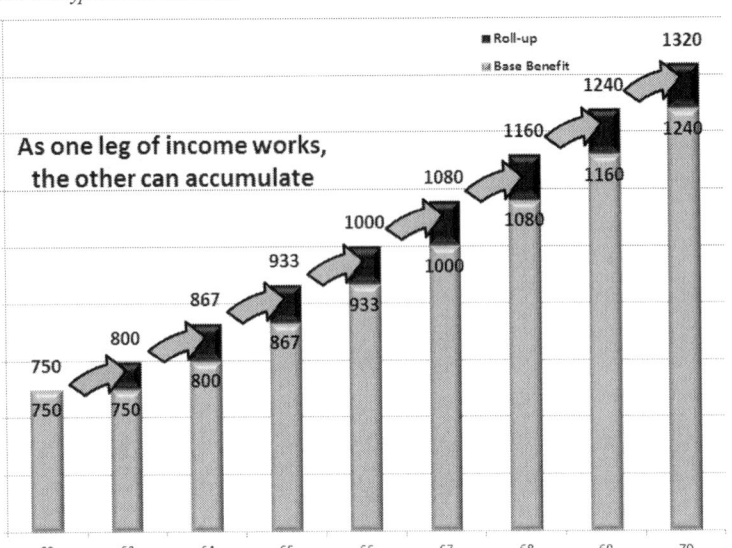

Roll-up is the guaranteed annual rate at which the income base grows.
The Base Benefit will determine the amount of future guaranteed income payments.

In order to encourage investors to leave their money in their annuity contracts, insurance companies create surrender periods that protect their investments. If you remove your money from the annuity contract during the surrender period, you will pay a penalty and will not be able to receive your entire investment amount back. A typical surrender period is 10 years. If after three years you decide that you want your $100,000 back, the insurance company has that money tied up in bonds and other investments with the understanding that they will have it for another seven years. Because they may take a hit on removing the money from their investments prematurely, you will have to pay a surrender charge that makes up for their loss. During the surrender period, an annuity is not a demand deposit account like a savings or checking account. The higher returns that you are guaranteed from an annuity are dependent on the timeframe you selected. The longer an insurance company can hold your money, the easier it is for them to guarantee a predictable return on it.

If you leave your money in the annuity contract, you get a reliable monthly income no matter what happens in the market. Once the surrender period has expired, you can remove your money whenever you want. Your money becomes liquid again because the insurance company has used it in an investment that fit the timeline of your surrender period. For many people, this is an attractive trade off that can provide a creative solution for filling their income gap.

When is an annuity with an income rider right for you? A good financial professional can help you make that determination by taking the time to listen closely to your situation and understanding what your needs are as you enter retirement. Every salesperson has a bag full of brochures and PowerPoint presentations, but they need to know exactly what the financial concerns of their individual clients are in order to help them make the most informed and beneficial decisions. Some people need income today; others need it in five or 10 years. Others may have their income needs met but are planning to move closer to their children and will need to buy a house in 10 years. Or, if you want income in 15 years, you might want to choose a different investment product for 10 years, and then switch to an annuity with an income rider during the last five years of your timeline. Everyone's situation is different and everyone's needs are different. People who are interested in annuities, however, usually need to make decisions that affect their income needs, whether it is filling their income gap, or providing for income down the road.

What happens if you place a shorter timeframe on those assets from which you need to draw an income? Something called single premium immediate annuities may be for you:

SINGLE PREMIUM IMMEDIATE ANNUITIES (SPIA)

A single premium immediate annuity is simply a contract between you and an insurance company. SPIAs are structured so that you pay a lump sum of money (a single premium) to an insurance company, and they give you a guaranteed income over an agreed upon time period. That time period could be five years, or it could be for the remainder of your lifetime. Guarantees from insurance companies are based on the claims-paying ability of the issuing insurance company.

SPIAs provide investors with a stream of reliable income when they can't afford to take the risk of losing money in a fluctuating market. While there is general faith that the market always trends up, at least in the long-term, if you are focusing on income over a shorter period of time, you may not be able to take a big hit in the market. Beyond normal market volatility, interest rates also come with an inherent level of uncertainty, making it hard to create a dependable income on your own. SPIAs reduce risk for you by giving you regular monthly, quarterly or yearly payments that can begin the moment you buy the contract. Your financial professional can walk you through a series of different payment options to help you select the one that most closely fits your needs.

Additional Annuity Information:
- Some contracts will allow you to draw income from the high water mark that the market reaches each year. The income rider will then begin calculating its value from the high water mark.
- Variable annuities, however, can lose money with market fluctuations. As their name suggests, they vary with the market. These annuities do not take advantage of annual reset when the market goes down. The income rider will stay the same, but the value of your actual contract may fall. If you surrender the annuity, the insurance company will pay you the market value of the asset, regardless of whether it matches, exceeds or falls short of the value at which you bought the contract. If its value has dropped significantly, you may be better off taking the income rider without surrendering your contract.

Managing Risk Within Your Annuity:
Just like any investment strategy, the amount of risk needs to fit the comfort level of the investor. Annuities are no exception. Without going into too much detail, here are some additional ways to manage risk with annuity options:
- If you want to structure an annuity investment for growth over a long period of time, you can select a variable annuity. The value of your principal investment follows the market and can lose or gain value with the market. This type of annuity can also have an income rider, but it is really more useful as an accumulation tool that bets on an improving market. A 40-year-old couple, for example, will probably want to structure more for growth and take on more risk than someone in their 70s. The 40-year-old couple may select a variable annuity with an income rider that kicks in when they plan to retire. If it rises with the

market or outperforms it, the value of their investment has grown. If the market loses ground over the duration of the contract or their annuity underperforms, they can still rely on the income rider.

- If you are 68 years old and you have more immediate income needs that you need to come up with above and beyond your Social Security, you need a low risk, reliable source of income. If you choose an annuity option, you are looking for something that will pay out an income right away over a relatively short timeframe. You probably want to opt for a SPIA that pays you immediately and spans a five year period, as well as an additional annuity that begins paying you in five years, and another longer term annuity that begins paying you in 10 years. Bear in mind that each annuity contract has its own costs and fees. Review these with your financial professional before you determine the best products and strategies for your situation.
- **Variable Annuity Alert!** If you are in the wrong type of variable annuity, you may be paying much higher fees than you have to. Save thousands of dollars and reduce your risk by requesting what is known as a *variable annuity analysis report*. Many reputable agencies offer these reports for free. **What they do is identify all the fees you are paying against the returns you have received.** This may be followed by a recommendation of other better annuities designed to increase your return and lower your fees.

The following example shows just how helpful an indexed annuity option can be for a retiree:

» *Kris and Martha are 62 years old and have decided to run the numbers to see what their retirement is going to look like. They know they currently need $6,000 per month to pay their bills and maintain their current lifestyle. They have also done their Social Security homework and have determined that, between the two of them, they will receive $4,200 per month in benefits. They also receive $350 per month in rent from a tenant who lives in a small carriage house in their backyard. Between their Social Security and the monthly rent income, they will be short $1,450 per month.*

They do have an additional asset, however. They have been contributing for years to an IRA that has reached a value of $350,000. They realize that they have to figure out how to turn the $350,000 in their IRA into $1,450 per month for the rest of their life. At first glance, it may seem like they will have plenty of money. With some quick calculations, they find they have 240 months, or nearly 20 years, of monthly income before they exhaust the account. When you consider income tax, the potential for higher taxes in the future, and market fluctuations (because many IRAs are invested in the market), the amount in the IRA seems to have a little less clout. Every dollar Kris and Martha take out of the IRA is subject to income tax, and if they leave the remainder in the IRA, they run the risk of losing money in a volatile market. Once they retire and stop getting a paycheck every two weeks, they also stop contributing to their IRA. And when they aren't supplementing its growth with their own money, they are entirely dependent on market growth. That's a scary prospect. They could also withdraw the money from the IRA and put it in a savings account or CD, but removing all the money at once will put them in a tax bracket that will claim a huge portion of the value of the IRA. A seemingly straightforward asset has now become a complicated equation. Kris and Mar-

tha didn't know what to do, so they met with their financial professional.

Their financial professional suggested that they use the money to purchase an indexed annuity with an income rider. They selected an annuity that was designed for their specific situation. They took the lump sum from their IRA, placed it in an indexed annuity taking advantage of annual reset so they never lost the value of their investment. In return, they were guaranteed the $1,450 of income per month that they needed to meet their retirement goals. The simplicity of the contract allowed them to do an analysis with their professional just once to understand the product. They basically put their money in an investment crockpot where they didn't have to look at it or manage it. They just needed to let it simmer. In fact, their professional was able to find an annuity for them that allowed them their $1,450 monthly payment with a lump sum of $249,455, leaving them more than $100,000 to reinvest somewhere else. Keep in mind that annuities are tax deferred, meaning you will pay tax on the income you receive from an annuity in the year you receive it. To save money on taxes you may want to consider a qualified indexed annuity.

PUTTING IT ALL TOGETHER

Designing an income plan before you retire allows you to satisfy your need for lifetime income and ensures that your lifestyle can last as long as you do. Design a plan that operates in the most efficient way possible and don't be afraid of options such as annuities that have gotten a bad reputation over the years. Annuities can give more security to your Need Later Money and will potentially allow you to build your legacy down the road.

Here is a basic roadmap of what we have covered so far:
- Review your income needs and look specifically at the shortfall you may have during each year of your retirement based on your Social Security income, and income from any other assets you have.
- Ask yourself where you are in your distribution phase. Is retirement one year away? 10 years away? Last year?
- Determine how much money you need and how you need to structure your existing assets to provide for that need.
- If you have an asset from which you need to generate income, consider options offered by purchasing an income rider on an annuity.

CHAPTER 5 RECAP //

- Annuities can form an important part of your retirement income plan by offering a green "safe money" option with a higher rate of interest than the standard bank rate. As an investment tool, they look and feel a bit like Social Security, offering you a way to grow your money while receiving a steady income.
- You can get all of your money out of the annuity after the surrender charge period unless you have purchased an immediate annuity with a lifetime option.
- Most annuities carry a provision that allows for a 10 percent free withdrawal annual of your entire balance.
- Understanding what an annuity can do for YOU is more important than understanding exactly how they work.
- Be sure you understand the features, benefits, costs and fees associated with any annuity product before you invest.

6

EARNING MONEY BY SAVING MONEY:
UNDERSTANDING RETIREMENT INCOME TAX

"What is counted as taxable income?"

Taxes play a starring role in the theater of retirement planning. Everyone is familiar with taxes (you've been paying them your entire working life), but not everyone is familiar with how to make tax planning a part of their retirement strategy.

Taxes are taxes, right? You'll pay them before retirement and you'll pay them during retirement. What's the difference?

***Tax planning* and *tax reporting* are two very different things**. Most people only *report* their taxes. March rolls around, people pull out their 1040s or use TurboTax to enter their income and taxable assets, and ship it off to Uncle Sam at the IRS. If you use a CPA to report your taxes, you are essentially paying them to record history. You have the option of being proactive with your taxes and to plan for your future by making smart, informed decisions about how taxes affect your overall financial plan. Working with a financial professional who, along with a CPA, makes recommendations about your finances to you, will keep you looking forward instead of in the rearview mirror as you enter retirement.

TAXES AND RETIREMENT

It is one thing to get a good rate of return on your accumulated retirement investments, but it's another thing if you lose 30 to 50 percent of that in taxes. We want to take a holistic approach when it comes to financial planning. This means not just considering the risk and return on what you save, but looking at how much you net *after* tax. In other words, **tax planning** takes a look at the actual dollars you can take home and spend.

When you retire, you move from the earning and accumulation phase of your life into the asset distribution phase of your life. For most people, that means relying on Social Security, a 401(k), an IRA, or a pension. Wherever you have put your Green Money for retirement, you are going to start relying on it to provide you with the income that once came as a paycheck. **Most of these distributions will be considered income by the IRS and will be taxed as such.** There are exceptions to that (not all of your Social Security income is taxed, and income from Roth IRAs is not taxed), but for the most part, your distributions will be subject to income taxes.

> » *Bill and Rhonda have a happy problem. They each have a pension which will bring in a combined total of $4,000 of income each month during their retirement. Rhonda's Social Security benefit adds another $700 month and Bill's will bring in another $1,200. But they also have a 401(k) and bank CD's valued at $350,000. They're going to have a pretty nice income when all of this adds up, but as a result, their*

Social Security income is going to be taxed at the highest rate — a whopping 85 percent! From a Social Security taxation standpoint, the IRS looks at all income sources and uses that to count against your Social Security taxation. In this case, the interest income earned by their 401(k) — also known as unearned income — is counting against Bill and Rhonda.

When their financial professional asks them about their tax plan, they tell him their CPA handled their taxes every year, and did a great job. Their professional says, "I don't mean who does your taxes, I mean, who does your tax planning?" Bill and Rhonda weren't sure how to respond.

Their professional brings Bill and Rhonda's financial plan to the firm's CPA and has her run a tax projection for them. A week later their professional calls them with a tax plan for the year that will save them more than $6,000 on their tax return. The couple is shocked. The financial professional recommended minimizing the unearned interest income from their 401(k) by focusing that money differently. If part of the $350,000 were repositioned into a tax deferred account where they wouldn't receive a 1099, then all of a sudden their taxable income drops. Another simple piece of advice from the CPA based on the numbers revealed that if they paid their estimated taxes before the end of the year, they would be able to itemize it as a deduction, allowing them to save even more.

While you can't alter or affect the dollar amount of your Social Security benefit, you can control HOW MUCH TAX YOU PAY on that benefit. This solution won't work for everyone, and it may not work for Bill and Rhonda every year. That's not the point. By being proactive with their approach to taxes and using the resources made available by their financial professional, they were able to create a tax plan that allowed them to save money by keeping more of the money they had already earned.

THE DISTRIBUTION PHASE

Regarding assets that you have in an IRA or a 401(k) plan, when you reach 70 ½ years of age, you will be required to draw a certain amount of money from your IRA as income each year. That amount depends on your age and the balance in your IRA. The amount that you are required to withdraw as income is called a Required Minimum Distribution (RMD). Why are you required to withdraw money from your own account? Chances are the money in that account has grown over time, and the government wants to collect taxes on that growth.

If you have a large balance in an IRA, there's a chance your RMD could increase your income significantly enough to put you into a higher tax bracket. This subjects more of your Social Security benefit to taxation, and ultimately means less income for you. So what options do you have?

You can't do anything about the RMD from an IRA or a 401(k). There are steep penalties for not taking your mandatory withdrawal, so you don't have a choice there. **What you *can* do is look at any other income that you have such as money in the bank, money tied up in CDs, or funds in a money market savings account. Any dividends or capital gains that are bumping up your income could be put into a tax deferred investment which could help to eliminate or minimize the income taxes on your Social Security income.**

Here's where the paradigm shift of retirement kicks in to another level. **The distribution phase of your life is about protecting your income, not earning more income.** This is where tax planning becomes a maximizing force that can work strongly in your favor. Your predictable income is based on your RMDs, your Social Security benefit and any other income-generating assets you may have. That income will be taxed, resulting in less net dollars in your pocket. So the question becomes, which is more important? The gross income or the net income?

Before retirement, showing a healthy income was desirable for a lot of reasons, such as building credit and qualifying for mortgage loans. If you're going to make $100,000 a year, you're going to be feeling pretty good, even if you only net $80,000 after taxes. Living on a fixed income, however, you might feel different. You might not be too happy about a 20 percent income loss due to taxes, especially if this loss is preventable.

Here's another way to look at it: If you had the opportunity to earn a bonus $25,000 a year during your retirement years, or the option of saving $25,000 a year in taxes, which would you pick?

While it might be tempting to jump at the additional $25,000 income, this choice wouldn't amount to more dollars in your pocket. Why not? These two choices aren't equal because if you make the additional $25,000 in income, you have to pay taxes on it. Not only that, the raise could effectively boost you into a higher income tax bracket, making things even worse. On the other hand, saving $25,000 on taxes goes right to your bottom line. It's more money in your pocket. And during your retirement years, that's where it matters most.

BUILDING A TAX DIVERSIFIED PORTFOLIO

So far so good: avoid taxes, maximize your net annual income and have a plan for doing it. When people decide to leverage the experience and resources of a financial professional, they may not be thinking of how distribution planning and tax planning will benefit their portfolios. Often more exciting prospects like planning income annuities, investing in the market and structuring investments for growth rule the day. Taxes, however, play a crucial role in retirement planning. Achieving those tax goals requires knowledge of options, foresight and professional guidance.

Finding the path to a good tax plan isn't always a simple task. Every tax return you file is different from the one before it because things constantly change. Your expenses change. Planned or unplanned purchases occur. Health care costs, medical bills, an inheritance, property purchases, reaching an age where your RMD kicks in or travel, any number of things can affect how much income you report and how many deductions you take each year.

Preparing for the ever-changing landscape of your financial life requires a tax-diversified portfolio that can be leveraged to balance the incomes, expenditures and deductions that affect you each year. A financial professional will work with you to answer questions like these:

- What does your tax landscape look like?
- Do you have a tax-diversified portfolio robust enough to adapt to your needs?
- Do you have a diversity of taxable and non-taxable income planned for your retirement?
- Will you be able to maximize your distributions to take advantage of your deductions when you retire?
- Is your portfolio strong enough and tax-diversified enough to adapt to an ever-changing (and usually increasing) tax code?

> *» When Beth returns home after a week in the hospital recovering from a knee replacement, the 77-year-old calls her daughter, sister and brother to let them know she is home and feeling well. She also should have called her CPA. Beth's medical expenses for the procedure, her hospital stay, her medications and the ongoing physical therapy she attended amount to more than $50,000.*
>
> *Currently, Americans can deduct medical expenses that account for more than 7.5 percent of their Adjusted Gross*

> Income (AGI). At the time of her hospital stay, Beth's AGI is $60,000, meaning she is able to deduct $44,000 of her medical bills from her taxes that year. Although her AGI dictated that she could deduct more than 80 percent of her medical expenses that year, **Beth didn't know this**.
>
> Had she been working with a financial professional who regularly asked her about any changes in her life, her spending, or her expenses (expected or unexpected), Beth could have saved thousands of dollars. If she does receive financial counsel, Beth does have the option of filing an amendment to her tax return to recoup the overpayment.

This relatively simple example of how tax planning can save you money is just the tip of the iceberg. No one can be expected to know the entire U.S. tax code. But a professional who is working with a team of CPAs and financial professionals have an advantage over the average taxpayer who must start from square one on their own every year. Have you been taking advantage of all the deductions that are available to you?

PROACTIVE TAX PLANNING

The implications of proactive tax planning are far reaching, and are larger than many people realize. Remember, doing your taxes in January, February, March or April means you are writing a history book. Planning your taxes in October, November or December means that you are writing the story as it happens. You can look at all the factors that are at play and make decisions that will impact your tax return *before* you file it.

When you incorporate tax planning into your financial planning strategy, it becomes part of the way you maximize your financial potential. Paying less in taxes means you keep more of your money. This kind of planning can affect you at any stage of your life, but as it relates to retirement, having a relationship with a professional who works with a CPA can help you build a truly comprehensive financial plan. Ideally, this plan not only works with your investments, but also shapes your assets to find the most efficient ways to prepare for tax time. There may be years that you could benefit from higher distributions because of the tax bracket that you are in, or there could be years you would benefit from taking less. There may be years when you have a lot of deductions and years you have relatively few. **Adapting your distributions to work in concert with your available deductions** is at the heart of smart tax planning. Professional guidance can bring you to the next level of income distribution, allowing you to remain flexible enough to maximize your tax efficiency. And remember, saving money on taxes makes you more money than making money does.

What you have on paper is important: your assets, savings, and investments, which are the financial expression of your work and time. It's just as important to know how to get it off the paper in a way that keeps most of it in your pocket. Almost anything that involves financial planning also involves taxes. Annuities, investments, IRAs, 401(k)s, 403(b)s, and many other investment options will have tax implications. Life also has a way of throwing curveballs. Illness, expensive car repair or replacement, or *any event that has a financial impact on your life will likely have a corresponding tax implication* around which you should adapt your financial plan. Tax planning does just that.

One dollar can end up being less than 25 cents to your heirs.

> » When Cal's father passed away, he discovered that he was the beneficiary of his father's $500,000 IRA. Cal has a wife and a family of four children, and he knew that his father had intended for a large portion of the IRA to go toward funding their college educations. After Cal's father's estate is

> distributed, Cal, who is 50 years old and whose two oldest sons are entering college, liquidates the IRA. By doing so, his taxable income for that year puts him in a 39.6 percent tax bracket, immediately reducing the value of the asset to $302,000. An additional 3.8 percent surtax on net investment income further diminishes the funds to $283,000. Liquidating the IRA in effect subjects much of Cal's regular income to the surtax, as well. At this point, Cal will be taxed at 43.4 percent. Cal's state taxes are an additional 9 percent. Moreover, estate taxes on Cal's father's assets claim another 22 percent. By the time the IRS is through, Cal's income from the IRA will be taxed at 75 percent, leaving him with $125,000 of the original $500,000. While it would help contribute to the education of his children, it wouldn't come anywhere near completely paying for it, something the $500,000 could have easily done.

As the above example makes clear, leaving an asset to your beneficiaries can be more complicated than it may seem. In the case of a traditional IRA, after federal, estate and state taxes, the asset could literally diminish to as little as 25 percent of its value.

How does working with a professional help you make smarter tax decisions with your own finances? Any financial professional worth their salt will be working with a firm that has a team of trained tax professionals, including CPAs, who have an intimate knowledge of the tax code and how to adapt a financial plan to it.

YELLOW MONEY AND TAXES

There are also tax implications for the money that you have managed professionally. People with portions of their investment portfolio that are actively traded can particularly benefit from having a proactive tax strategy. Without going into too much detail, for tax purposes there are two kinds of investment money: qualified and non-qualified. Different investment strategies can have different effects on how you are taxed on your investments and the growth of your investments. Some are more beneficial for one kind of investment strategy over another. Determining how to plan for the taxation of non-qualified and qualified investments is fodder for holiday party discussions at accounting firms. While it may not be a stimulating topic for the average investor, you don't have to understand exactly how it works in order to benefit from it.

While there are many differences between qualified and non-qualified investments, the main difference is this: qualified plans are designed to give investors tax benefits by deferring taxation of their growth until they are withdrawn. Non-qualified investments are generally not eligible for these deferral benefits. As such, non-qualified investments are taxed whenever income is realized from them in the form of growth. One exception to this rule is the annuity, which offers tax deferral,

Actively and non-actively traded investments provide a simple example of how to position your investments for the best tax advantage. In an actively traded and managed portfolio, there is a high amount of buying and selling of stocks, bonds, funds, ETFs, etc. If that active portfolio of non-qualified investments does well and makes a 20 percent return one year and you are in the 39.6 percent tax bracket, your net gain from that portfolio is only about 12 percent (39.6 percent tax of the 20 percent gain is roughly 8 percent.) In a passive trading strategy, you can use a qualified investment tool, such as an IRA, to achieve 13, 14 or 15 percent growth (much lower than the actively traded portfolio), but still realize a higher net return because the growth of the qualified investment is not taxed until it is withdrawn.

Does this mean that you have to always rely on a buy and hold strategy in qualified investment tools? Not necessarily. The question is, if you have qualified and non-qualified investments, where do you want to position your actively traded and managed assets? Incorporating a planful approach to positioning your investments for more beneficial taxation can be done many ways, but let's consider one example. Keeping your actively managed investment strategies inside an IRA or some other qualified plan could allow you to realize the higher gains of those investments without paying tax on their growth every year. Your more passively managed funds could then be kept in taxable, non-qualified vehicles and methods, and because you aren't realizing income from them on an annual basis by frequently trading them, they grow sheltered from taxation.

If you are interested in taking advantage of tax strategies that maximize your net income, you need the attentive strategies, experience and knowledge of a professional who can give you options that position you for profit. At the end of the day, what's important to you as the consumer is how much you keep, your after-tax take home.

ESTATE TAXES

The government doesn't just tax your income from investments while you're alive. They will also dip into your legacy. While estate taxes aren't as hot of a topic as they were a few years ago, they are still an issue of concern for many people with assets. While taxes may not apply on estates that are less than $5 million, certain states have estate taxes with much lower exclusion ratios. Some are as low as $600,000. Many people may have to pay a state estate tax. One strategy for avoiding those types of taxes is to move assets outside of your estate. That can include gifting them to family or friends, or putting them into an irrevocable trust. Life insurance is another option for protecting your legacy.

CHAPTER 6 RECAP //

- Tax planning during retirement isn't the same thing as tax preparation. During your retirement years, tax planning looks at the amount of dollars you get to keep in your pocket.
- Retirement is the distribution phase of your life, during which the amount of money that you net is more important than the amount of money that you gross.
- Tax planning can directly affect your beneficiaries, costing them or saving them hundreds of thousands of dollars.
- Talk with your financial advisor about the tax implications regarding yellow money – the money that you have in managed funds – to give you options that position you for profit.

7
THE BRANDEIS STORY
"Should I convert my IRA?"

Louis Brandeis provides one of the best examples illustrating how tax planning works. Brandeis was Associate Justice on the Supreme Court of the United States from 1916 to 1939. Born in Louisville, Kentucky, Brandeis was an intelligent man with a touch of country charm. He described tax planning this way:

"I live in Alexandria, Virginia. Near the Court Chambers, there is a toll bridge across the Potomac. When in a rush, I pay the dollar toll and get home early. However, I usually drive outside the downtown section of the city and cross the Potomac on a free bridge.

The bridge was placed outside the downtown Washington, D.C. area to serve a useful social service – getting drivers to drive the extra mile and help alleviate congestion during the rush hour.

If I went over the toll bridge and through the barrier without paying a toll, I would be committing tax evasion.

*If I drive the extra mile and drive outside the city of Washington to the free bridge, I am using a legitimate, logical and suitable method of tax avoidance, and I am performing a useful social service by doing so. The tragedy is that **few people know that the free bridge exists.**"*

Like Brandeis, most American taxpayers have options when it comes to "crossing the Potomac," so to speak. It's a financial planner's job to tell you what options are available. You can wait until March to file your taxes, at which time you might pay someone to report and pay the government a larger portion of your income. However, you could instead file before the end of the year, work with your financial professional and incorporate a tax plan as part of your overall financial planning strategy. Filing later is like crossing the toll bridge. Tax planning is like crossing the free bridge.

Which would you rather do?

The answer to this question is easy. Most people want to save money and pay less in taxes. What makes this situation really difficult in real life; however, is that the signs along the side of the road that direct us to the free bridge are not that clear. To normal Americans, and to plenty of people who have studied it, the U.S. tax code is easy to get lost in. There are all kinds of rules, exceptions to rules, caveats and conditions that are difficult to understand, or even to know about. What you really need to know is your options and the bottom line impacts of those options.

THE INCOME TAX DEBACLE

If we put two hundred people in a room together and asked the question, "How many of you think that income taxes will go up sometime in the next 20 years?" Most of the people in that room would raise their hand. If most people think that tax rates are only going to go up, wouldn't it make good sense to pay a lower tax *now* rather than a higher tax *later*?

The income tax debacle concerns the question of IRAs, and whether it's better to tuck away your money and pay the taxes later, as in a traditional IRA, or pay the taxes now, and withdraws the money later tax free, as offered by a Roth IRA. Another important difference between the accounts is how they treat Required Minimum Distributions (RMDs). When you turn 70 ½ years old, you are required to take a minimum amount of money out of a traditional IRA. This amount is your RMD. It is treated as taxable income. Roth IRAs, however, do not have RMDs, and their distributions are not taxable. Quite a deal, right?

If tax rates are lower now than they're going to be for the rest of our lives, why not pay those taxes now, at a discounted tax rate?

CONSIDER THE ROTH IRA

The main difference between a Roth and a traditional IRA or employer-sponsored plan lies in the timing of the taxation. We are all very familiar with the typical scenario of putting money away for retirement through an employer plan, whereby they deduct money from our paychecks and put it directly into a retirement account. **This money is taken out before taxes are calculated, meaning we do not pay tax on those earnings today.** This is how a traditional IRA works.

A Roth account, on the other hand, takes the money after the taxes have been removed and puts it into the retirement account, so we do pay tax on the money today. The other significant difference between these two is taxation during distribution in later years.

Regarding our traditional retirement accounts, when we take the money out later it is added to our ordinary income and is taxed accordingly. Additionally, including this in our income subjects us to the consequences mentioned above for municipal bonds with Social Security taxation, AMT, as well as higher Medicare premiums. A Roth on the other hand is distributed tax-advantaged and does not contribute toward negative impact items such as

Social Security taxation, AMT, or Medicare premium increases. It essentially comes back to us without tax and other obligations.

Converting some or all of a traditional IRA into a ROTH IRA is one way of "taking the free bridge" when it comes to income taxes and retirement. The big hurdle to get over is that you'll be paying a pretty good amount in taxes now, when you convert. Working with a financial professional, however, you might be able to finds a solution that helps to alleviate some of that tax burden.

> » *Mae is a single retiree with a traditional IRA valued at $300,000. After learning about the amount she would save in taxes by converting to a ROTH IRA, Mae made an appointment with a financial professional. Because she is living on a fixed income, she doesn't think she can afford to convert the entire amount now and pay what would amount to $30,000 in taxes. With her advisor, they looked at several options, including converting a portion of her IRA, and moving all of it into an annuity for safety. Converting $100,000 now would put Mae in a higher tax bracket, amounting to $30,000 in taxes. What this means to Mae's bottom line is that her $100,000 is now only worth $70,000. However, Mae's advisor found her an annuity that pays out a 10 percent bonus. By moving all $300,000 over to the annuity, and converting $100,000 of it to a ROTH IRA, the 10 percent bonus pays for the tax bill.*

Situations like Mae's require careful study. There are Roth IRA tax conversion analysis reports that can show you exactly what the tax conversion would cost, and what it would save over the life of your retirement.

By paying taxes now instead of later on assets in a Roth IRA, you can realize tax-advantaged growth. You pay once and you're done paying. Your heirs are done paying. It's a powerful tool.

While you have to pay a conversion tax to transfer your assets, you also have turned taxable income into tax free retirement money that you can let grow as long as you want without being required to withdraw it.

Here's another simple example to show you how powerful this tool can be:

Imagine that you pay to convert a traditional IRA to a Roth. You have decided that you want to put the money in a vehicle that gives you a tax-advantaged income option down the road. If you pay a 25 percent tax on that conversion and the Roth IRA then doubles in value over the next 10 years, you could look at your situation as only having paid 12.5 percent tax.

Your financial professional will likely tell you that it is not a matter of whether or not you should perform a Roth IRA conversion, it is a matter of how much you should convert and when.

Here are some of the things to consider before converting to a Roth IRA:

- If you make a conversion before you retire, you may end up paying higher taxes on the conversion because it is likely that you are in some of your highest earning years, placing you in the highest tax bracket of your life. It is possible that a better strategy would be to wait until after you retire, a time when you may have less taxable income, which would place you in a lower tax bracket.
- Many people opt to reduce their work hours from full-time to part-time in the years before they retire. If you have pursued this option, your income will likely be lower, in turn lowering your tax rate.
- The first years that you draw Social Security benefits can also be years of lower reported income, making it another good time frame in which to convert to a Roth IRA.

One key strategy to handling a Roth IRA conversion is to *always be able to pay the cost of the tax conversion with outside money,* as in the story above with Mae. Structuring your tax year to include something like a significant deduction can help you offset the conversion tax. This way you aren't forced to take the money you need for taxes from investment and are subject to depletion expenses, they can be deducted and used to offset a Roth IRA conversion tax. The reason taxes apply to this maneuver is because when you withdraw money from a traditional IRA, it is treated as taxable income by the IRS. Your financial professional, with the help of the CPAs at their firm, may be able to provide you with options like after-tax money, itemized deductions or other situations that can pose effective tax avoidance options.

Some examples of avoiding Roth IRA conversions taxes include:

- *Using medical expenses that are above 10 percent of your Adjusted Gross Income.* If you have health care costs that you can list as itemized deductions, you can convert an amount of income from a traditional IRA to a Roth IRA that is offset by the deductible amount. Essentially, deductible medical expenses negate the taxes resulting from recording the conversion.
- *Individuals, usually small business owners, who are dealing with a Net Operating Loss (NOL).* If you have NOLs, but aren't able to utilize all of them on your tax return. You can carry them forward to offset the taxable income from the taxes on income you convert to a Roth IRA.
- *Charitable giving.* If you are charitably inclined, you can use the amount of your donations to reduce the amount of taxable income you have during that year. By matching the amount you convert to a Roth IRA to the amount your taxable income was reduced by charitable giving, you

can essentially avoid taxation on the conversion. You may decide to double your donations to a charity in one year, giving them two years' worth of donations in order to offset the Roth IRA conversion tax on this year's tax return.
- *Investments that are subject to depletion.* Certain investments can kick off depletion expenses. If you make an investment and are subject to depletion expenses, they can be deducted and used to offset a Roth IRA conversion tax.

Not all of the above scenarios work for everyone as easily as they did for Mae, but there are many other options for offsetting conversion taxes. The point is that you have options. As you approach retirement you should consider your options and make choices that keep more of your money in your pocket, not the governments.

ADDITIONAL TAX BENEFITS OF ROTH IRAS

Not only do Roth IRAs provide you with tax-advantaged growth, they also give you a tax diversified landscape that allows you to maximize your distributions. Chances are that no matter the circumstances, you will have taxed income and other assets subject to taxation. **But if you have a Roth IRA, you have the unique ability to manage your Adjusted Gross Income (AGI), because you have a tax-advantaged income option!**

Converting to a Roth IRA can also help you preserve and build your legacy. Because Roth IRAs are exempt from RMDs, after you make a conversion from a traditional IRA, your Roth account can grow tax-advantaged for another 15, 20 or 25 years and it can be used as tax-advantaged income by your heirs. It is important to note, however, that non-spousal beneficiaries do have to take RMDs from a Roth IRA, or choose to stretch it and draw tax-advantaged income out of it over their lifetime.

TO CONVERT OR NOT TO CONVERT?

Conversions aren't only for retirees. You can convert at any time. Your choice should be based on your individual circumstances and tax situation. Sticking with a traditional IRA or converting to a Roth, again, depends on your individual circumstances, including your income, your tax bracket and the amount of deductions you have each year.

Is it better to have a Roth IRA or traditional IRA? It depends on your individual circumstance. Some people don't mind having taxable income from an IRA. Their income might not be very high and their RMD might not bump their tax bracket up, so it's not as big a deal. A similar situation might involve income from Social Security. Social Security benefits are taxed based on other income you are drawing. If you are in a position where none or very little of your Social Security benefit is subject to taxes, paying income tax on your RMD may be very easy.

> » *There are also situations where leveraging taxable income from a traditional IRA can work to your advantage come tax time. For example, Darrel and Bobbi-Jo dream of buying a boat when they retire. It is something they have looked forward to their entire marriage. In addition to the savings and investments that they created to supply them with income during retirement, which includes a traditional IRA, they have also saved money for the sole purpose of purchasing a boat once they stop working.*
>
> *When the time comes and they finally buy the boat of their dreams, they pay an additional $15,000 in sales taxes that year because of the large purchase. Because they are retired and earning less money, the deductions they used to be able to realize from their income taxes are no longer there. The high amount of sales taxes they paid on the boat puts them in a*

position where they could benefit from taking taxable income from a traditional IRA.

When Darrel and Bobbi-Jo's financial professional learns about their purchase, he immediately contacts a CPA at his firm to run the numbers. They determine that by taking a $15,000 distribution from their IRA, they could fulfill their income needs to offset the $15,000 sales tax deduction that they were claiming due to the purchase of their boat. In the end, they pay zero taxes on their income distribution from their IRA.

The moral of the story? **Having a tax diversified landscape gives you options.** Having capital assets that can be liquidated, tax-advantaged income options and sources that can create capital gains or capital losses will put you in a position to play your cards right no matter what you want to accomplish with your taxes. The ace up your sleeve is your financial professional and the CPAs they work with. Do yourself a favor and *plan* your taxes instead of *reporting* them!

CHAPTER 7 RECAP //
- Look for the "free bridge" option in your tax strategy.
- The future of U.S. taxation is uncertain. You know what the tax rate and landscape is today, but you won't tomorrow. The only thing you can really count on is the trend of increasing taxation.
- Converting from a traditional to a Roth IRA can provide you with tax-advantaged retirement income.
- Work with a financial professional to discover ways to make converting to a Roth IRA doable by using sources of outside money to fund the tax payment that comes as part of the conversion fee.

8
THE FUTURE OF U.S. TAXATION

If you were one of the people who raised your hand in response to the question, "How many people think taxes will go up?" a brief look at American history will further prove you right. The process of raising taxes takes several years to go from planning to implementation. Understanding why this is so and gaining insight into the process can help you make better choices when considering tax-advantaged options for your retirement savings.

DEBT CEILING – CAUSE AND EFFECTS
The raising of the debt ceiling raised more than just the ability for our government to go further into debt. It also raised concerns and fears about the future of our economy. We are now seeing major swings in the markets with investors showing serious concerns over the future of investment valuations and their personal wealth. Unfortunately, the reasoning behind all of this uncertainty is preceded by the inability to see the full implications

of what is in store. We rarely talk about the fact that the discussions on raising the debt ceiling were coupled to discussions on major tax reforms needed to correct the problems underlying the debt ceiling increase itself.

Increasing the debt ceiling was needed because the government maxed out its credit card, so to speak, which it has been living off of for quite some time. It is really not much different than what we have been seeing from the general public for the past few decades. Unfortunately, most of us do not have the ability to get a credit limit increase on our credit cards once we reach the maximum limit, that is unless we can show the ability to pay this balance back. The only way to pay this credit card back is by spending less and making more money.

This is exactly where the federal government is today. They have been given a higher credit limit, but they still must find a way to decrease the spending while making more money. The only way the government makes money is by collecting taxes.

Unfortunately, at the current moment, the government is collecting approximately $120 billion less per month than it currently spends. Discussions for major tax reform have accompanied the discussions for the increased debt ceiling.

DEBT AND EARNINGS

Let us take a closer look at where we are today. The U.S. national debt is increasing at an alarming rate, rising to levels never seen before and threatening serious harm to the economy. Through the end of 2010, the national debt has risen to $13.6 trillion, averaging an 11.4 percent increase annually over the past five years and a 9.2 percent increase annually over the past 10 years. To put this into perspective, the national gross domestic product (GDP) has increased to $14.5 trillion during the same period, averaging a 2.9 percent annual increase over the past five years and a 3.9 percent increase over the past 10 years. At the end of 2010, the national debt level was 93 percent of the GDP. Economists believe that a sustainable economy exists at a maximum level of approximately 80 percent. As of December 20, 2013, the U.S. national debt is 107.69 percent of GDP with the debt at $17.252 trillion and the GDP at $16.020 trillion.*

The significance of these two numbers lies within the contrast. The national debt is the amount that needs to be repaid. This is the credit card balance. Gross domestic product on the other hand is less known and represents the market value of all final goods and services produced within a country during a given period. Essentially, GDP represents the gross taxable income avail- able to the government. If debts are increasing at a greater rate than the gross income available for taxation, then the only way to make up the difference is by increasing the rate at which the gross income is taxed.

The most recent presidential budget shows a continuing trend in the disparity between growth in the national debt and GDP over the next two decades. Although the increasing disparity is a real concern and shows that, at least in the short run, the federal deficit will not be addressed to counteract the potential crisis ahead, it is the revenue collection that tells the disconcerting story. Over the past 40 years the average collection of GDP has been approximately 17.6 percent and currently collections are at approximately 14.4 percent of GDP.

As the presidential budget reveals, the projected revenues are estimated to be 20 percent by the end of the next decade. That is a 38.8 percent increase from the current tax levels. To put this into perspective, if you are currently in the top tax bracket of 35 percent and this bracket increases by the proposed collection increase, your tax rate will be approximately 48.5 percent. Keep in mind that even at this rate the deficit is projected to increase.

---

*http://www.usdebtclock.org/ 12/20/13

2013 – THE END OF AN ERA?

From a historical point of view, taxes are extremely low. The last time the U.S. national debt was at the same percentage level of GDP as today was at the end of World War II and several years following. The maximum tax rate averaged 90 percent from 1944 through 1963. Compare that to the maximum rate of 35 percent today and it becomes very clear that there is a disparity of extreme proportion.

Taxes during this historical period were at extreme levels for nearly 20 years, during and following this current level of debt-to-GDP. A significant point to note about the difference between that time and today is the economic activity. The period of 1944 through 1963 was in the heart of both the industrial revolution and the birth of the Baby Boom generation. Today, we are mired in extreme volatility with frequent periods of boom and bust at the same time we are witnessing the beginning of the greatest retirement wave ever experienced within the U.S. economy.

To contrast these two time periods in respect to the recovery period is almost asinine as the external pressures from globalization and domestic unfunded liabilities did not exist or were irrelevant factors during the prior period.

To add insult to injury, U.S. domestic unfunded liabilities are currently estimated somewhere around $61.6 trillion due to items such as Social Security, Medicare and government pensions. The most concerning part of this pertains to the coming wave of retirement as the Baby Boom generation begins retiring and drawing on the unfunded Social Security for which they currently have entitlement. Over the long run, expenditures related to healthcare programs such as Medicare and Medicaid are projected to grow faster than the economy overall as the population matures.

To put unfunded liabilities into perspective, consider these as off-balance-sheet obligations similar to those of Enron. Although these are not listed as part of the national debt, they must be paid. These liabilities exist outside of the annual budgetary debt discussed. The difference between Enron and the U.S. unfunded liabilities is that if the U.S. government cannot come up with the funds to pay all these liabilities through revenue generation, they will print the money necessary to pay the debt.

WHAT DOES THE SOLUTION LOOK LIKE?

Unfortunately, the general public is in a no-win situation for this solution to the problem. Printing money does not bode well for economic growth. This creates inflationary pressures that devalue the U.S. dollar and make everyone less wealthy. Cutting the entitlements that compose this liability leaves millions of people without benefits they have come to expect. The only other option, and one that the government knows all too well, is increasing taxes. In fact, according to a Congressional Budget Office paper issued in 2004:

"The term 'unfunded liability' has been used to refer to a gap between the government's projected financial commitment under a particular program and the revenues that are expected to be available to fund that commitment. But no government obligation can be truly considered 'unfunded' because of the U.S. government's sovereign power to tax – which is the ultimate resource to meet its obligations."

A balanced budget will be required at some point and with this will come higher taxes. We have uncertainty surrounding tax rates and how high they will go. At that time, extensions put in place in December 2010 on Bush-era tax cuts are set to expire. We are likely to see some tax increases at this point. Whether it is only on the top earners or unilaterally across all income levels is yet to be seen, but an increase of some sort will most certainly occur.

How do you prepare? Why spend so much time reassuring you that taxes will increase? Because you have an opportunity to take action. **Now is the time to prepare for what will come and** structure countermeasures for the good, the bad and the ugly of each of these legislative nightmares through tax-advantaged retirement planning.

As discussed earlier in Chapter Six, you make more money by saving on taxes than you do by making more money. As simple as this sounds, it is much more difficult to execute. Most people fail to put together a plan as they near retirement, beginning with a simple cash flow budget. If you have not analyzed your proposed income streams and expenses, you could not possibly have taken the time to position these cash flows and other events into a tax-preferred plan.

Most people will state that they have a plan and, thus, do not need any further assistance in this area. The truth in most instances is that people could not show you their plan, and among the few that could, most would not be able to show you how they have executed it. In this regard, they might as well be Richard Nixon stating, "I am not a crook" for as much as they state, "I have a plan." The truth lies in waiting. As we approach or begin retirement, we should look at what cash flows we will have. Do we have a pension? How about Social Security? How much additional cash flow am I going to need to draw from my assets to maintain the lifestyle that I desire?

We spend our whole lives saving and accumulating wealth but spend so little time determining how to distribute this accumulation so as to retain it. We need to make sure we have the appropriate diversification of taxable versus non-taxable assets to complement our distribution strategy.

THE BENEFITS OF DIVERSIFICATION

Heading into retirement, we should be situated with a diversified tax landscape. The point to spending our whole lives accumulating wealth is not to see the size of the number on paper, but rather to be an exercise in how much we put in our pocket after re- moving

it from the paper. To truly understand tax diversification, we must understand what types of money exist and how each of these will be treated during accumulation and, most importantly, during distribution. The following is a brief summary:
1. Free money
2. Tax-advantaged money
3. Tax-deferred money
4. Taxable money
    a. Ordinary income
    b. Capital gains and qualified dividends

FREE MONEY

Free money is the best kind of money regardless of tax treatment because, in the end, you have more money than you would have otherwise. Many employers will provide contributions toward employee retirement accounts to offer additional employment benefits and encourage employees to save for their own retirement. With this, employers often will offer a matching contribution in which they contribute up to a certain percentage of an employee's salary (generally three to five percent) toward that employee's retirement account when the employee contributes to their retirement account as well. For example, if an employee earns $50,000 annually and contributes three percent ($1,500) to their retirement account annually, the employer will also contribute three percent ($1,500) to the employee's account. That is $1,500 in free money. Take all you can get! Bear in mind that any employer contribution to a 401(k) will still be subject to taxation when withdrawn.

TAX-ADVANTAGED MONEY

Tax-advantaged money is the next best thing to free money. Although you have to earn tax-advantaged money, you do not have to give part of it away to Uncle Sam. Tax-advantaged money comes in three basic forms that you can utilize during your lifetime; (four if prison inspires your future,) but we are not going to discuss that option.

One of the most commonly known forms of tax-advantaged money is municipal bonds, which earn and pay interest that could be tax-advantaged on the federal level, or state level, or both. There are several caveats that should be discussed with regard to the notion of tax-advantaged income from municipal bonds. First, you will notice that tax-advantaged has several flavors from the state and federal perspective. This is because states will generally tax the interest earned on a municipal bond unless the bond is offered from an entity located within that state. This severely limits the availability of completely tax-advantaged municipal bonds and constrains underlying risk and liquidity factors. Second, municipal bond interest is added back into the equation for determining your modified adjusted gross income (MAGI) for Social Security. This could push your income above a threshold and subject a portion of your Social Security income to taxation. In effect, if this interest subjects some other income to taxation then this interest is truly being taxed.

Last, municipal bond interest may be excluded from the regular federal tax system, but it is included for determining tax under the alternative minimum tax (AMT) system. In its basic form, the AMT system is a separate tax system that applies if the tax computed under AMT exceeds the tax computed under the regular tax system. The difference between these two computations is the alternative minimum tax.

TAX-ADVANTAGED MONEY: ROTH IRA

Roth accounts are probably the single greatest tax asset that has come from Congress outside of life insurance. They are well known but rarely used. Roth IRAs were first established by the Taxpayer Relief Act of 1997 and named after Senator William

Roth, the chief sponsor of the legislation. Roth accounts are simply an account in the form of an individual retirement account or an employer sponsored retirement account that allows for tax-advantaged growth of earnings and, thus, tax-advantaged income.

The best way to view the difference between a traditional and a Roth IRA accounts is to look at the life of a farmer. A farmer will buy seed, plant it in the ground, grow the crops and harvest it later for sale. Typically, the farmer would only pay tax on the crops that have been harvested and sold. But if you were the farmer, would you rather pay tax on the $5,000 of seed that you plant today or the $50,000 of crops harvested later? The obvious answer is $5,000 of seed today. The truth to the matter is that you are a farmer, except you plant dollars into your retirement account instead of seeds into the earth.

So why doesn't everyone have a Roth retirement account if things are so simple? There are several reasons, but the single greatest reason has been the constraints on contributions. If you earned over certain thresholds (MAGI over $125,000 single and $183,000 joint for 2012), you were not eligible to make contributions, and until last year, if your modified adjusted gross income (MAGI) was over $100,000 (single or joint), you could not convert a traditional IRA to a Roth. Outside these contribution limits, most people save for retirement through their employers and most employers do not offer Roth options in their plans. The reason behind this is because Roth accounts are not that well understood and people have been educated to believe that saving on taxes today is the best possible course of action.

TAX-ADVANTAGED MONEY: LIFE INSURANCE

As previously mentioned, the single greatest tax asset that has come from Congress outside of life insurance is the Roth account. Life insurance is the little-known or little-discussed tax asset that holds some of the greatest value in your financial history both during life and upon death. It is by far the best tax-advantaged device available. We traditionally view life insurance as a way to protect our loved ones from financial ruin upon our demise and it should be noted that everyone who cares about someone should have life insurance. Purchasing a life insurance policy ensures that our loved ones will receive income from the life insurance company to help them pay our final expenses and carry on with their lives without us comfortably when we die. The best part of the life insurance windfall is the fact that nobody will have to pay tax on the money received. This is the single greatest tax-advantaged device available, but it has one downside, we do not get to use it. Only our heirs will.

The little known and discussed part of life insurance is the cash value build-up within whole life and universal life (permanent) policies. Life insurance is not typically seen as an investment vehicle for building wealth and retirement planning, although we should discuss briefly why this thought process should be re-evaluated. Permanent life insurance is generally misconceived as something that is very expensive for a wealth accumulation vehicle because there are mortality charges (fees for the death benefit) that detract from the available returns. Furthermore, those returns do not yield as much as the stock market over the long run. This is why many times you will hear the phrase "buy term and invest the rest," where "term" refers to term insurance.

Let us take a second to review two terms just used in regard to life insurance: term and permanent. Term insurance is an idea with which most people are familiar. You purchase a certain death benefit that will go to your heirs upon death and this policy will be in effect for a certain number of years, typically 10 to 20 years. The 10 to 20 years is the term of the policy and once you have reached that end you no longer have insurance unless you purchase another policy.

Permanent insurance on the other hand has no term involved. It is permanent as long as the premiums continue to be paid. Permanent insurance generally initially has higher premiums than term insurance for the same amount of death benefit coverage and it is this difference that is referred to when people say "invest the rest."

Simply speaking there are significant differences between these two policies that are not often considered when providing a comparative analysis of the numbers. One item that gets lost in the fray when comparing term and permanent insurance is that term usually expires before death. In fact, insurance studies show less than one percent of all term policies pay out death benefit claims. The issue arises when the term expires and the desire to have more insurance is still present.

A term policy with the same benefit will be much more expensive than the original policy and, many times, life events occur, such as cancer or heart conditions, which makes it impossible to acquire another policy and leaves your loved ones unprotected and tax-advantaged legacy planning out of the equation.

Another aspect and probably the most important piece in consideration of the future of taxation is the fact that permanent insurance has a cash accumulation value. Two aspects stand out with the cash accumulation value. First, as the cash accumulation value increases the death benefit will also increase whereas term insurance remains level. Second, this cash accumulation offers value to you during your lifetime rather than to your heirs upon death. The cash accumulation value can be used for tax-advantaged income during your lifetime through policy loans. Most importantly, this tax-advantaged income is available during retirement for distribution planning, all while offering the same typical financial protection to your heirs.

TAX-DEFERRED MONEY

Tax-deferred money is the type of money with which most of people are familiar, but we also briefly reviewed the idea above. Tax-deferred money is typically our traditional IRA, employer sponsored retirement plan or a non-qualified annuity. Essentially, you put money into an investment vehicle that will accumulate in value over time and you do not pay taxes on the earnings that grow these accounts until you distribute them. Once the money is distributed, taxes must be paid. However, the same negative consequences exist with regard to additional taxation and expense in other areas as previously discussed. The cash accumulation value can be used for tax-advantaged income.

TAXABLE MONEY

Taxable money is everything else and is taxable today, later or whenever it is received. These four types of money come down to two distinct classifications: taxable and tax-free. The greatest difference when comparing taxable and tax-advantaged income is a function of how much money we keep after tax. For help in determining what the differences should be, excluding outside factors such as Social Security taxation and AMT, a tax equivalent yield should be used.

TAX-ADVANTAGED IN THE REAL WORLD

To give you a clearer picture of what tax equivalent yields look like when put into practice by real people, consider the following situation:

> » *Denise and Lavon are currently retired, living on Social Security and interest from investments and falling within the 25 percent tax bracket. They have a substantial portion of their investments in municipal bonds yielding 6 percent, which is quite comforting in today's market. The tax equiva-*

lent yield they would need to earn from a taxable investment would be 8 percent, a 2 percent gap that seems almost impossible given current market volatility. However, something that has never been put into perspective is that the interest from their municipal bonds is subject to taxation on their Social Security benefits (at 21.25 percent). With this, the yield on their municipal bonds would be 4.725 percent, and the taxable equivalent yield falls to 6.3 percent, leaving a gap of only 1.575 percent.

In the end, most people spend their lives accumulating wealth through the best, if not the only vehicle they know, a tax-deferred account. This account is most likely a 401(k) or 403(b) plan offered through our employer and may be supplemented with an IRA that was established at one point or another. As the years go by, people blindly throw money into these accounts in an effort to save for a retirement that we someday hope to reach.

The truth is, most people have an age selected for when they would like to retire, but spend their lives wondering if they will ever be able to actually quit working. To answer this question, you must understand how much money you will have available to contribute toward your needs. **In other words, you need to know what your after-tax income will be during this period.**

All else being equal, it would not matter if you put your money into a taxable, tax-deferred or tax-advantaged account as long as income tax rates never change and outside factors are never an event. The net amount you receive in the end will be the same. Unfortunately, this will never be the case. We already know that taxes will increase in the future, meaning we will likely see higher taxes in retirement than during our peak earning years.

Regardless, saving for retirement in any form is a good thing as it appears from all practical perspectives that future government benefits will be cut and taxes will increase. You have the ability to plan today for efficient tax diversification and maximization of our after-tax dollars during your distribution years.

CHAPTER 8 RECAP //
- A closer examination of the debt-ceiling and taxes throughout U.S. history points to the benefits of tax diversification.
- Most people are familiar with tax-deferred methods of retirement savings such a traditional IRAs. By taking action now, you can prepare for the rise in taxes by restructuring your assets to include the benefits of free and tax-advantaged money.
- Tax-advantaged money is money you earn without having to pay taxes on. One of the most common forms includes interest on municipal bonds, but be aware these come with many state and federal caveats and complexities.
- Roth IRAs and Life Insurance are two forms of tax-advantaged money that can take advantage of today's lower tax rate when preparing for tomorrow's retirement.

THE IMPACT OF VOLATILITY ON THE INDIVIDUAL INVESTOR

"Can you take another hit?"

Katie's situation illustrates how market volatility can have major repercussions for an individual investor. Katie worked as an Executive Assistant to a major construction firm in Arkansas for 34 years. During her time there, she acquires bonuses and pay raises that often include shares of stock in the company. She also dedicates part of her paycheck every month to a 401(k) that bought stock in the construction company. By the time she retires, Katie has $250,000 worth of the construction company's stock.

Although she had contributes to her 401(k) account every month, Katie doesn't cultivate any other assets that could generate income for her during retirement. Katie also retires early at age 62 because of her failing health. The commute to work every day was becoming difficult in her weakened condition and she wanted to enjoy the rest of her life in retirement instead of working at Acme.

Because she retires early, Katie fails to maximize her Social Security benefit. While she lives a modest lifestyle, her income needs will still be $3,500 per month. Katie's monthly Social Security check will only cover $1,900, leaving her with a $1,600 income gap. To supplement her Social Security check, Katie sells $1,600 of her Acme stock each month to meet her income needs. A $250,000 401(k) is nothing to sneeze at, but reducing its value by $1,600 every month will barely last Katie 10 years. And that's if the market stays neutral or grows modestly. If the market takes a downturn, the money that Katie relied on to fill her income gap will rapidly diminish. Even if the market starts going up in a couple of years, it will take much larger gains for her to recover the value that she lost.

Unhappily for Katie, she retired in 2007, just before the major market downturn that lasted for several years. She lost more than 20 percent of the value of her stock. Because Katie needed to sell her stock to meet her basic income needs, the market price of the stock was secondary to her need for the money. When she needed money, she was forced to sell however many shares she needed to fill her income gap that month. And if she has a financial crisis, involving her need for medical care, for example, she will be forced to sell stock even if the market is low and her shares are nearly worthless.

Katie realizes that she could have relied on an investment structured to deliver her a regular income while protecting the value of her investment. She could have kept her $250,000 from diminishing while enjoying her lifestyle into retirement regardless of the volatility of the market. Ideally, Katie would have restructured her 401(k) to reflect the level of risk that she was able to take. In her case, she would have had most of her money in Green Money assets, allowing her to rely on the value of her assets when she needed them.

People are less apt to make a change until they feel pain. As long as things are going along just fine, it's all too easy to not do anything. As soon as the stock market changes, however, and the market values of your stocks start to dwindle, the tendency is to make sudden or abrupt changes that negatively affect the stability of your retirement income.

EMOTIONS AND YOUR BOTTOM LINE

In 2013, DALBAR, the well-respected financial services market research firm, released their annual "Quantitative Analysis of Investment Behavior" report (QAIB). The report studied the impact of market volatility on individual investors: people like Katie, or anyone who was managing (or mismanaging) their own investments in the stock market.

According to the study, volatility not only caused investors to make decisions based on their emotions, those decisions also harmed their investments and prevented them from realizing potential gains. So why do people meddle so much with their investments when the market is fluctuating? Part of the reason is that many people have financial obligations that they don't have control over. Significant expenses like house payments, the unexpected cost of replacing a broken-down car, and medical bills can put people in a position where they need money. If they need to sell investments to come up with that money, they don't have the luxury of selling when they *want* to. They must sell when they *need* to.

DALBAR's "Quantitative Analysis of Investor Behavior" has been used to measure the effects of investors' buying, selling and mutual fund switching decisions since 1994. The QAIB shows time and time again over nearly a 20 year period that the average investor earns less, and in many cases, significantly less than the performance of mutual funds suggests. QAIB's goal is to improve independent investor performance and to help financial professionals provide helpful advice and investment strategies that address the concerns and behaviors of the average investor.

An excerpt from the report claims that:

"QAIB offers guidance on how and where investor behaviors can be improved. No matter what the state of the mutual fund industry, boom or bust: Investment results are more dependent on investor behavior than on fund performance. Mutual fund investors who hold on to their investments are more successful than those who time the market.

QAIB uses data from the Investment Company Institute (ICI), Standard & Poor's and Barclays

Capital Index Products to compare mutual fund investor returns to an appropriate set of benchmarks.

There are actually three primary causes for the chronic shortfall for both equity and fixed income investors:

1. *Capital not available to invest. This accounts for 25 percent to 35 percent of the shortfall.*
2. *Capital needed for other purposes. This accounts for 35 percent to 45 percent of the shortfall.*
3. *Psychological factors. These account for 45 percent to 55 percent of the shortfall."*

The key findings of Dalbar's QAIB report provide compelling statistics about how individual investment strategies produced negative outcomes for the majority of investors:

- Psychological factors account for 45 percent to 55 percent of the chronic investment return shortfall for both equity and fixed income investors.
- Asset allocation is designed to handle the investment decision-making for the investor, which can materially reduce the shortfall due to psychological factors.
- Successful asset allocation investing requires investors to act on two critical imperatives:

1. Balance capital preservation and appreciation so that they are aligned with the investor's objective.
2. Select a qualified allocator.

- The best way for an investor to determine their risk tolerance is to utilize a risk tolerance assessment. However, these assessments must be accessible and usable.
- Evaluating allocator quality requires analysis of the allocator's underlying investments, decision making process and whether or not past efforts have produced successful outcomes.
- Choosing a top allocator makes a significant difference in the investment results one will achieve.
- Mutual fund retention rates suggest that the average investor has not remained invested for long enough periods to derive the potential benefits of the investment markets.
- Retention rates for asset allocation funds exceed those of equity and fixed income funds by over a year.
- Investors' ability to correctly time the market is highly dependent on the direction of the market. Investors generally guess right more often in up markets. However, in 2012 investors guessed right only 42 percent of the time during a bull market.
- Analysis of investor fund flows compared to market performance further supports the argument that investors are unsuccessful at timing the market. Market upswings rarely coincide with mutual fund inflows while market downturns do not coincide with mutual fund outflows.
- Average equity mutual fund investors gained 15.56 percent compared to a gain of 15.98 percent that just holding the S&P 500 produced.
- The shortfall in the long-term annualized return of the average mutual fund equity investor and the S&P 500 continued to decrease in 2012.

- The fixed-income investor experienced a return of 4.68 percent compared to an advance of 4.21 percent on the Barclays Aggregate Bond Index.
- The average fixed income investor has failed to keep up with inflation in nine out of the last 14 years.*

It doesn't take a financial services market research report to tell you that market volatility is out of your control. The report does prove, however, that before you experience market volatility, you should have an investment plan, and when the market is fluctuating, you should stand by your investment plan.

CHAPTER 9 RECAP //

- More than the behavior of the stock market, it is the behavior of you, the investor, which impacts your bottom line the most.
- A holistic approach to investing includes a review of not just your financial circumstances, but your goals, health, and risk tolerance.
- A bad economy and a volatile market can cause investors to feel anxious and vulnerable. Without a plan and the guidance of a tax professional, investors acting alone can make changes to their portfolios that negatively affect their bottom line.
- Financial planners don't try to outsmart the market when managing investments for their clients. Instead, they tap into the potential for gains by committing to proven and long-term investment strategies.

*2013 QAIB, Dalbar, March 2013

10
YELLOW MONEY AND YOUR RETIREMENT

"What should I do with the rest of my money?"

Before we continue along the road to financial success, let's take a brief look at what we've covered so far. Your goals and pressing concerns formed the basis for our starting point. Organizing your assets into colors based on their corresponding levels of risk increased the chances that you will get to keep more of the money you've worked so hard to earn. We looked at Green Money options such as annuities for filling in any gaps between the income you have and the income you need; we talked about how to balance your financial needs against the tax issues – both today's and tomorrow's – of drawing on benefits such as Social Security, 401(k)s and IRAs. You've now reached a crossroads where it's time to look at ways to utilize the Need Later Money portion of your funds in a safe, Red Money way.

PLAYING WITH FIRE

How much of your Red Money should you invest, and in what kinds of markets, investment products, and stocks? What kind of factors allow for the greatest accumulations? And how will you know when to take your money out of a fund that appears to be underperforming?

The stock market is clearly the place to go for greater accumulation, but dealing with stock market volatility is a lot like playing with fire. The previous chapter outlining the DALBAR report and its findings spoke to your chances of getting burned by the market as an individual investor playing it alone. Mr. and Mrs. Average Investor failed to keep up with inflation during 9 out of the last 14 years, but failing to invest means not keeping up with inflation. Does the risk of outliving your money outweigh the risks of playing the stock market?

There is another option: Yellow Money. Maximize the earning-power of your stocks, mutual funds and other investment products can be done by relying on the experience and knowledge of a trusted financial professional. Red Money managed by a financial professional can magically transform a fire-red risk into an easy-going gold.

FOLLOW THE YELLOW-BRICK ROAD

Yellow Money is money that is managed by a professional *with a purpose*. It is still considered a type of Red Money, but there is a dedicated direction, strategy, and end-goal in mind. Like following the yellow brick road to the Emerald City, working with a financial professional to manage growth-funds increases the chances that you'll be seeing more "green."

To take the analogy even further, consider how Dorothy's chances of success improved once she met the Scarecrow, the Tinman, and the Lion. Making the journey alone exposed her to more risk from the elements, not to mention the Wicked Witch of the West. Managing your money alone or through a stockbroker means there is very limited active management going on, a.k.a. – no yellow-brick road to walk upon, and no friends to walk with. Money is deposited in lump sums in a variety of mutual funds or stocks, and you "hope" for the best. Unless your broker is also an investment advisor, what typically happens is that when a big drop or loss in your account occurs, the only advice you'll get is something along the lines of, "Don't worry about the market drop, it will always come back." And the reason they say that is because they don't have a proactive plan or strategy to fix what's broken. Managed money is still at risk – the forest is full of lions and tigers and bears, after all – but you have a team of professionals with you. They are working with you to make decisions based on the best way to protect your account.

WHAT WILL IT COST ME?

Think about your investment portfolio. Think specifically of what you would consider your Red Money. Do you know what is there? You may have several different investment products like individual mutual funds, bond accounts, stocks, etc. You may have inherited a stock portfolio from a relative, or you might be invested in a bond account offered by the company for which you worked due to your familiarity with them. While you may or may not be managing your investments individually, the reality is that you probably don't have an overall management strategy for all of your investments.

For some people, the idea of paying someone to manage money is off-putting, even though there is a fundamental difference in way the accounts are managed. **Ironically, the fees that scare people are often times not any different than what they are already paying to their stockbrokers, yet with managed money, they're getting so much more.** In other cases, the fees are a higher, but when you look at the returns and the lower risks, it's clearly worth it. Here's why:

Investments that aren't managed are simply Red Money, or money that is at risk in the market. Harnessing the earning potential of your Red Money relies on more than a collection of stocks and bonds; it needs guided management. A good Yellow Money manager uses the knowledge they have about the level of risk with which you are comfortable, what you need or want to use your money for, and when you want or need it. The Yellow Money options that they present to you will still have a certain level of risk, but under the right management, control and process, you have a far better chance of a successful outcome that meets your specific needs.

When you sit down with an investment professional, you can look at all of your assets together. Chances are that you have accumulated a number of different assets over the last 20, 30 or 50 years. You may have a 401(k), an IRA, a Roth IRA, an account of self-directed stocks, a brokerage account, etc. Wherever you put your money, a financial professional will go through your assets and help you determine the level of risk to which you are exposed now and should be exposed in the future.

Here is a typical example of how an investment professional can be helpful to a future retiree with Yellow Money needs:

> » *Beverly is 65 years old and wants to retire in two years. She has a 401(k) from her job to which she has contributed for 26 years. She also has some stocks that her late husband man- aged. Beverly also has $55,000 in a mutual fund that her sister recommended to her five years ago and $30,000 in another mutual fund that she heard about at work. She takes a look at her assets one day and decides that she doesn't understand what they add up to or what kind of retirement*

they will provide. She decides to meet with an investment professional. Beverly's professional immediately asks her:

1. Does she know exactly where all of her money is? *Beverly doesn't know much about all her husband's stocks, which have now become hers. Their value is at $100,000 invested in three large cap companies. Beverly is unsure of the companies and whether she should hold or sell them.*

2. Does she know what types of assets she owns? *Yes and no. She knows she had a 401(k) and IRAs, but she is unfamiliar with her husband's self-directed stock portfolio or the type of mutual funds she owns. Furthermore she is unclear as to how to manage the holdings as she nears retirement.*

3. Does she know the strategies behind each one of the investment products she owns? *While Beverly knows she had a 401(k), an IRA and mutual fund holdings, she doesn't know how her 401(k) is organized or how to make it more conservative as she nears retirement. She is unsure whether her IRA is a Roth or traditional variety and how to draw income from them? She really does not have specific investment principles guiding her investment decisions, and she doesn't know anything about her husband's individual stocks. One major concern for Beverly is whether her family would be okay if she were not around.*

After determining Beverly's assets, her financial professional prepares a consolidated report that lays out all of her assets for her to review. Her professional explains each one of them to her. Beverly discovers that although she is two years away from retiring, her 401(k) is organized with an amount of risk with which she is not comfortable. Sixty percent of her 401(k) is at risk, far off the mark if we abide by the Rule of 100. Beverly opts to be more conservative than the Rule of 100 suggests, as she will rely on her 401(k) for most of her immediate income needs after retirement. Beverly's professional also points out several instances of overlap between her mutual funds. Beverly learns that while she is comfortable with one of her mutual funds, she does not agree with the management principles of the other. In the end, Beverly's professional helps her reorganize her 401(k) to secure her more Green Money for retirement income. Her professional also uses her mutual fund and her husband's stock assets to create a growth oriented investment plan that Beverly will rely on for Need Later Money in 15 years when she plans on relocating closer to her children and grandchildren. By creating an overall investment strategy, Beverly is able to meet her targeted goals in retirement. Beverly's financial professional worked closely with her and her tax professional to minimize the tax impact of any asset sales on Beverly's situation.

Like Beverly, you may have several savings vehicles: a 401(k), an IRA to which you regularly contribute some mutual funds to which you make monthly contributions, etc. But what is your *overall investment strategy*? Do you have one in place? Do you want one that will help you meet your retirement goals? Yellow Money looks at *ALL* your accounts and all their different strategies to create a plan that helps them all work together. Your current investment situation may not reflect your wishes. As a matter of fact, it likely doesn't.

AVOIDING EMOTIONAL INVESTING

There's no way around it; people get emotional about their money. And for good reason. You've spent your life working for it, exchanging your time and talent for it, and making decisions about how to invest it, save it and make it grow. The maintenance of your lifestyle and your plans for retirement all depend on it. The best investment strategies, however, don't rely on emotions.

One of Yellow Money's greatest strengths lies in the fact that it is managed by someone who understands your needs and desires, but doesn't make decisions about your money under the influence of emotion.

A well-managed investment account meets your goals as a whole, not in individualized and piecemeal ways. Professional money managers do this by creating requirements for each type of investment in which they put your money. We'll call them "screens." Your money manager will run your holdings through the screens they have created to evaluate different types of investment strategies. A professionally managed account will only have holdings that meet the requirements laid out in the overall management plan that was designed to meet your investment goals. The holdings that don't make it through the screens, the ones that don't contribute to your investment goals, are sold and redistributed to investments that your financial professional has determined to be appropriate.

Different screens apply to different Yellow Money strategies. For example, if one of your goals is significant growth, which would require taking on more risk alongside the potential for more return, an investment professional would screen for companies that have high rates of revenue and sales growth, high earnings growth, rising profit margins, and innovative products. On the other hand, if you want your portfolio to be used for income, which would call for lower risk and less return, your professional would screen for dividend yield and sector diversification. *Every investor has a different goal, and every goal requires a customized strategy that uses quantitative screens.* A professional will create a portfolio that reflects your investment desires. If some of the current assets you own complement the strategies that your professional recommends, those will likely stay in your portfolio.

Screening your assets removes emotions from the equation. It removes attachment to underperforming or overly risky investments. Financial professionals aren't married to particular stocks or mutual funds for any reason. They go by the numbers and see your portfolio through a lens shaped by your retirement goals. Your professional understands your wants and needs, and creates an investment strategy that takes your life events and future plans into account. It's a planful approach, and it allows you to tap into the tools and resources of a professional who has built a career around successful investing. Managing money is a full time job and is best left to a professional money manager.

Removing emotions from investing also allows you to be unaffected by the day-to-day volatility of the market. Your financial professional doesn't ask where the market is going to be in a year, three years or a month from now. If you look at the value of the stock market from the beginning of the twentieth century to today, it's going up. Despite the Great Depression, despite the 1987 crash, despite the 2008 market downturn, the market, as a whole, trends up. Remember the major market downturn in 2008 when the market lost 30 percent of its value? Not only did it completely recover, it has far exceeded its 2008 value. Emotional investing led countless people to sell low as the market went down, and buy the same shares back when the market started to recover. That's an expensive way to do business. While you can't afford to lose money that you need in two, three or five years, your Need Later Money has time to grow. The best way to do so is to make it Yellow.

CREATING AN INVESTMENT STRATEGY

Just like Beverly and Oscar, chances are that you can benefit from taking a more managed investment approach tailored to your goals. Yellow Money is generally Need Later Money that you want to grow for needs you'll have in at least 10 years. You can work with your financial planner to identify investments that meet your needs within different timeframes. You may need to rely on some of your Yellow Money in 10, 15 or 20 years, whether for additional income, a large purchase you plan on making or a vacation. Whatever you want it for, you will need it down the road.

So what does a Yellow Money account look like? Here's what it *doesn't* look like: a portfolio with 49 small cap mutual funds, a dozen individual stocks and an assortment of bond accounts. A brokerage account with a hodgepodge of investments, even if goal-oriented, is not a professionally managed account. It's still Red Money. Remember, Yellow Money is a managed account that has an overarching investment philosophy. When you look at making investments that will perform to meet your future income needs, the burning question becomes: How much should you have in the market and how should it be invested? Working with a professional will help you determine how much risk you should take, how to balance your assets so they will meet your goals and how to plan for the big ticket items, like health care expenses, that may be in your future. Yes, Yellow Money is exposed to risk, but by working with a professional, you can manage that risk in a productive way.

WHY YELLOW MONEY?

If you have met your immediate income needs for retirement, why bother with professionally managing your other assets? The money you have accumulated above and beyond your income needs probably has a greater purpose. It may be for your children or grandchildren. You may want to give money to a charity or organization that you admire. In short, you may want to craft your legacy. It would be advantageous to grow your assets in the best manner possible. A financial professional has built a career around managing money in profitable ways. They are experts under the supervision of the organization that they represent.

Turning to Yellow Money also means that you don't have to burden yourself with the time commitment, the stress, and the cost of determining how to manage your money. Yellow Money can help you better enjoy your retirement. Do you want to sit down in your home office every day and determine how to best allocate your assets, or do you want to be living your life while someone else manages your money for you? When the majority of your Red Money is managed with a specific purpose by a financial professional, you don't have to be worrying about which stocks to buy and sell today or tomorrow.

SEEKING FINANCIAL ADVICE: STOCK BROKERS VS. INVESTMENT ADVISOR REPRESENTATIVES

Investors basically have access to two types of advice in today's financial world: advice from stock brokers and advice given by investment advisors. Most investors, however, don't know the difference between types of advice and the people from whom they receive advice. Today, there are two primary types of advice offered to investors: advice given by a commission-based registered representative (brokers) and advice given by fee-based Investment Advisor Representatives. Unfortunately, many investors are not aware that a difference exists; nor have they been explained the distinction between the two types of advice. In a survey taken by TD Ameritrade, the top reasons investors choose to work with an independent registered investment advisor are:*

- Registered Investment Advisors are required, as fiduciaries, to offer advice that is in the best interest of clients
- More personalized service and competitive fee structure offered at a Registered Investment Advisor firm
- Dissatisfaction with full commission brokers

The truth is that there is a great deal of difference between stock brokers and investment advisor representatives. For starters, investment advisor representatives are obligated to act in an investor's best interests in every and all aspect of a financial relationship. Confusion continues to exist among investors struggling to find

---

*2011 Advisor Sentiment Study, commissioned by TD AMERITRADE. TD Ameritrade, Inc.

the best financial advice out there and the most credible sources of advice.

Here is some information to help clear up the confusion so you can find good advice from a professional you can trust:

- Investment advisor representatives have the fiduciary duty to act in a client's best interest at all times with every investment decision they make. Stock brokers and brokerage firms usually do not act as fiduciaries to their investors and are not obligated to make decisions that are entirely in the best interest of their customers. For example, if you decide you want to invest in precious metals, a stock broker may offer you a precious metals account from their firm. An Investment Advisor would find you a precious metals account that is the best fit for you based on the investment strategy of your portfolio.
- Investment advisors give their clients a Form ADV describing the methods that the professional uses to do business. An Investment Advisor also obtains client consent regarding any conflicts of interest that could exist with the business of the professional.
- Stock brokers and brokerage firms are not obligated to provide comparable types of disclosure to their customers.
- Whereas stock brokers and firms routinely earn large profits by trading as principal with customers, Investment Advisors cannot trade with clients as principal (except in very limited and specific circumstances).
- Investment Advisors charge a pre-negotiated fee with their clients in advance of any transactions. They cannot earn additional profits or commissions from their customers' investments without prior consent. Registered Investment Advisors are commonly paid an asset-based fee that aligns their interests with those of their clients. Brokerage firms and stock brokers, on the other hand, have much different

payment agreements. Their revenues may increase regardless of the performance of their customers' assets.
- Unlike brokerage firms, where investment banking and underwriting are commonplace, Registered Investment Advisors must manage money in the best interests of their customers. Because Registered Investment Advisors charge set fees for their services, their focus is on their client. Brokerage firms may focus on other aspects of the firm that do not contribute to the improvement of their clients' assets.
- Unlike brokers, Fee Only Registered Investment Advisors do not get commissions from fund or insurance companies for selling their investment products.

Just to drive home the point, here is what a fiduciary duty to a client means for a Registered Investment Advisor. Registered Investment Advisors must:*

- Always act in the best interest of their client and make investment decisions that reflect their goals.
- Identify and monitor securities that are illiquid.
- When appropriate, employ fair market valuation procedures.
- Observe procedures regarding the allocation of investment opportunities, including new issues and the aggregation of orders.
- Have policies regarding affiliated broker-dealers and maintenance of brokerage accounts.
- Disclose all conflicts of interest.
- Have policies on use of brokerage commissions for research.
- Have policies regarding directed brokerage, including step-out trades and payment for order flow.
- Abide by a code of ethics.

---

*2011 Advisor Sentiment Study, commissioned by TD AMERITRADE. TD Ameritrade, Inc.

// CHAPTER 10 RECAP

- Yellow Money is money that is managed by a professional with a purpose. It is still considered a type of Red Money, but there is a dedicated direction, strategy, and end-goal in mind which makes it less dangerous than an unmanaged portfolio.
- Like following the yellow-brick road, choosing to have your money managed gives you both direction and good company.
- Yellow Money takes the emotion out of investing. It frees you from the burden and stress of managing money, resulting in more peace of mind.
- There is a great deal of difference between stock brokers and investment advisor representatives, and even professionals themselves may not be aware of all the differences.

11
NEW IDEAS FOR INVESTING
"Does the safety of my money have to come at the expense of a return?"

In Chapter 1, we discussed how today's investment options require advice that is relevant to today. Traditional, outdated investment strategies are not only ineffective, they can be harmful to the average investor. One of the most traditional ways of thinking about investing is the risk versus reward trade-off. It goes something like this:

Investment options that are considered safer carry less risk, but also offer the potential for less return. Riskier investment options carry the burden of volatility and a greater potential for loss, but they also offer a greater potential for large rewards. Most professionals move their clients back and forth along this range, shifting between investments that are safer and investments that are structured for growth. Essentially, the old rules of investing dictate that you can either choose relative safety *or* return, but you can't have both.

Updated investment strategies work with the flexibility of liquidity to remake the rules. Here is how:

There are three dimensions that are inherent in any investment: *Liquidity, Safety,* and *Return*. You can maximize any two of these dimensions at the expense of the third. If you choose Safety and Liquidity, this is like keeping your assets in a checking account or savings account. This option delivers a lot of Safety and Liquidity, but at the expense of any Return. On the other hand, if you choose Liquidity and Return, meaning you have the potential for great return and can still reclaim your money whenever you choose, you will likely be exposed to a very high level of risk.

Understanding Liquidity can help you break the old Risk versus Safety trade-off. By identifying assets from which you don't require Liquidity, you can place yourself in a position to potentially profit from relatively safe investments that provide a higher than average rate of return.

Choosing Safety and Return over Liquidity can have significant impacts on the accumulation of your assets. In Ted's case, the paradigm shift from earning and saving to leveraging assets was a costly one.

> » *Ray is a corn and soybean farmer with 1,200 acres of land. He routinely retains somewhere between $40,000 and $80,000 in his checking and savings accounts. If a major piece of equipment fails and needs repair or replacement, Ray will need the money available to pay for the equipment and carry on with farming. If the price of feed for his cattle goes up one year, he will need to compensate for the increased overhead to his farming operation. He isn't a particularly wealthy farmer, but he has little choice but to keep a portion of money on hand in case something comes up and he must*

access it quickly. Most of his capital is held in livestock in the pasture or crops in the ground tied up for six to eight months of the year. When a major financial need arises, Ray can't just harvest 10 acres of soybeans and use them for payment. He needs to depend heavily on Liquidity in order to be a successful farmer.

Old habits die hard, however, and when Ray finally hangs up his overalls and quits farming, he keeps his bank accounts flush with cash, just like in the old days. After selling the farm and the equipment, Ray keeps a huge portion of the profits in Liquid investments because that's what he is familiar with. Unfortunately for Ray, with his pile of money sitting in his checking account, he isn't even keeping pace with inflation. After all his hard work as a farmer, his money is losing value every day because he didn't shift to a paradigm of leveraging his assets to generate income and accumulate value.

Almost anything would be a better option for Ray than clinging to Liquidity. He could have done something better to get either more return from his money or more safety, and at the very least would not have lost out to inflation.

As you can see, choosing Liquidity solely can be a costly option. The sooner you want your money back, the less you can leverage it for Safety or Return. If you have the option of putting your money in a long-term investment, you will be sacrificing Liquidity, but potentially gaining both Safety and Return. Rethinking your approach to money in this way can make a world of difference and can provide you with a structured way to generate income while allowing the value of your asset to grow over time.

The question is, how much Liquidity do you *really* need? Think about it. If you haven't sat down and created an income plan for your retirement, your perceived need for Liquidity is a guess. You don't know how much cash you'll need to fill the income gap if you don't know the amount of your Social Security benefit of the total of your other income options. If you *have* determined your income need and have made a plan for filling your income gap, you can partition your assets based on when you will need them. With an income plan in place, *you can use new rules to enjoy both Safety and Return from your assets.*

CHAPTER 11 RECAP //

- The three aspects of any investment include liquidity, safety, and return. You can choose to maximize any two against the third.
- Choosing to maximize liquidity alone can be an expensive option because the sooner you need your money back, the less you can leverage it for safety and return.

12
PREPARING YOUR LEGACY
"What difference have other people made in your life?"

If you're like most people, planning your estate isn't on the top of your list of things to do. Planning your income needs for retirement, managing your assets and just living your life without worrying about how your estate will be handled when you are gone make legacy planning less than attractive for a Saturday afternoon task. The fact of the matter, however, is that if you don't plan your legacy, someone else will. That someone else is usually a combination of the IRS and other government entities: lawyers, executors, courts, and accountants. Who do you think has the best interests of your beneficiaries in mind?

> » *Jim organized his assets long ago. He started planning his retirement early and made investment decisions that would meet his needs. With a combination of IRA to Roth IRA conversions, a series of income annuities and a well- planned*

money management strategy overseen by his financial professional, he easily filled his income gap and was able to focus on ways to accumulate his wealth throughout his retirement. He reorganized his Know So and Hope So Money as he got older. When Jim retired, he had an income plan created that allowed him to maximize his Social Security benefit. He even had enough to accumulate wealth during his retirement. At this point, Jim turned his attention to planning his legacy. He wanted to know how he could maximize the amount of his legacy he will pass on to his heirs.

Jim met with an attorney to draw up a will, but he quickly learned that while having a will was a good plan, it wasn't the most efficient way to distribute his legacy. In fact, relying solely on a will created several roadblocks.

The two main problems that arose for Jim were *Probate* and *Unintentional Disinheritance:*

Problem #1: Probate
Probate. Just speaking the word out loud can cause shivers to run down your spine. Probate's ugly reputation is well deserved. It can be a costly, time consuming process that diminishes your estate and can delay the distribution of your estate to your loved ones. Nasty stuff, by any measure. Unless you have made a clear legacy plan and discussed options for avoiding probate, it is highly likely that you have many assets that might pass through probate needlessly. ***If your will and beneficiary designations aren't correctly structured, some of these assets will go through the probate process, which can turn dollars into cents.***

If you have a will, probate is usually just a formality. There is little risk that your will won't be executed per your instructions. The problem arises when the costs and lengthy timeline that pro- bate creates come into play. Probate proceedings are notoriously expensive, lengthy and ponderous. A typical probate process identifies all of your assets and debts, pays any taxes and fees that you owe (including estate tax), pays court fees, and distributes your property and assets to your inheritors. This process usually takes at least a year, and can take even longer before your inheritors actually receive anything that you have left for them. For this reason, and because of the sometimes exorbitant fees that may be charged by lawyers and accountants during the process, probate has earned a nasty reputation.

Probate can also be a painstakingly public process. Because the probate process happens in court, the assets you own that go through a probate procedure become part of the public record. While this may not seem like a big deal to some, other people don't want that kind of intimate information available to the public.

Additionally, if your estate is entirely distributed via your will, the money that your family may need to cover the costs of your medical bills, funeral expenses and estate taxes will be tied up in probate, which can last up to a year or more. While immediate family members may have the option of requesting immediate cash from your assets during probate to cover immediate health care expenses, taxes, and fees, that process comes with its own set of complications. Choosing alternative methods for distributing your legacy can make life easier for your loved ones and can help them claim more of your estate in a more timely fashion than traditional methods.

A simpler and less tedious approach is to avoid probate altogether by structuring your estate to be distributed outside of the probate process. Two common ways of doing this are by structuring your assets inside a life insurance plan, and by using individual retirement planning tools like IRAs that give you the option of designating a beneficiary upon your death.

Problem #2: Unintentionally Disinheriting Your Family

You would never want to unintentionally disinherit a loved one or loved ones because of confusion surrounding your legacy plan. Unfortunately, it happens. Why? This terrible situation is typically caused by a simple lack of understanding. In particular, mistakes regarding legacy distribution occur with regards to those whom people care for the most: their grandchildren.

One of the most important ways to plan for the inheritance of your grandchildren is by properly structuring the distribution of your legacy. Specifically, you need to know if your legacy is going to be distributed *per stirpes* or *per capita*.

Per Stirpes. *Per stirpes* is a legal term in Latin that means "by the branch." The distribution of assets follows the family tree down the line as the predecessor beneficiaries pass away. Your estate will be distributed *per stirpes* if you designate each branch of your family to receive an equal share of your estate. In the event that your children predecease you, their share will be distributed evenly between their children — your grandchildren. Distributing your assets in this manner is as simple as writing on the beneficiary designation, "per stirpes," but you have to remember to do it.

Per Capita. *Per capita* distribution is different in that you may designate different amounts of your estate to be distributed to members of the same generation. **However, it can be easy to unintentionally disinherit your loved ones because per capita distribution of assets ends on the branch of the family tree with the death of a designated beneficiary.** For example, when your child passes away, in a per capita distribution, your grandchildren would not receive distributions from the assets that you designated to your child.

What these terms mean is not nearly as important as what they do. The reality is that improperly titled assets could accidentally leave your grandchildren disinherited upon the death of their parents. It's easy to check, and it's even easier to fix.

A simple way to remember the difference between the two types of distribution goes something like this: "***Stripes are forever and Capita is capped.***"

LIFE INSURANCE: AN IMPORTANT LEGACY TOOL

Another way to avoid complicated legacy distribution problems, and the probate process, is by leveraging a life insurance plan.

One of the most powerful legacy tools you can leverage is a good life insurance policy. Life insurance is a highly efficient legacy tool because it creates money when it is needed or desired the most. Over the years, life insurance has become less expensive, while it offers more features, and it provides longer guarantees.

There are many unique benefits of life insurance that can help your beneficiaries get the most out of your legacy. Some of them include:

- Providing beneficiaries with a tax-free, liquid asset.
- Covering the costs associated with your death.
- Providing income for your dependents.
- Offering an investment opportunity for your beneficiaries.
- Covering expenses such as tuition or mortgage down payments for your children or grandchildren.

Very few people want life insurance, but nearly everyone wants what it does. Life insurance is specifically, and uniquely, capable of creating money when it is needed most. When a loved one passes, no amount of money can remove the pain of loss. And certainly, money doesn't solve the challenges that might arise with losing someone important.

It has been said that when you have money, you have options. When you don't have money, your options are severely limited. You might imagine a life insurance policy can give your family and loved ones options that would otherwise be impossible.

> *Ethan spent the last 20 years building a small business. In so many ways, it is a family business. Each of his three children, Rebecca, Ella and Reuben worked in the shop part-time during high school. But after all three attended college, only Ella returned to join her father, and eventually will run the business full-time when Ethan retires.*
>
> *Ethan is able to retire comfortably on Social Security and on-going income from the shop, but the business is nearly his entire financial legacy. It is his wish that Ella own the business outright, but he also wants to leave an equal legacy to each of his three children.*
>
> *There is no simple way to divide the business into thirds and still leave the business intact for Ella.*
>
> *Ethan ends up buying a life insurance policy to make up the difference. Rebecca and Reuben will receive their share of an inheritance in cash from the life insurance policy and Ella will be able to inherit the business intact.*
>
> *Ethan is able to accomplish his goals, treat all three children equitably and leave Ella the business she helped to build.*

If you have a life insurance policy but you haven't looked at it in a while, you may not know how it operates, how much it is worth and how it will be distributed to your beneficiaries. You may also need to update your beneficiaries on your policy. In short, without a comprehensive review of your policy, you don't really know where the money will go or to whom it will go.

If you don't have a life insurance policy but are looking for options to maintain and grow your legacy, speaking with a professional can show you the benefits of life insurance. Many people don't consider buying a life insurance policy until some event in their life triggers it, like the loss of a loved one, an accident or a health condition.

BENEFITS OF LIFE INSURANCE

Life insurance is a useful and secure tool for contingency planning, ensuring that your dependents receive the assets that you want them to have, and for meeting the financial goals you have set for the future. While it bears the name "Life Insurance," it is, in reality, a diverse financial tool that can meet many needs. The main function of a life insurance policy is to provide financial assets for your survivors. Life insurance is particularly efficient at achieving this goal because it provides a tax-advantaged lump sum of money in the form of a death benefit to your beneficiary or beneficiaries. That financial asset can be used in a number of ways. It can be structured as an investment to provide income for your spouse or children, it can pay down debts, and it can be used to cover estate taxes and other costs associated with death.

Tax liabilities on the estate you leave behind are inevitable. Capital property, for instance, is taxed at its fair market value at the time of your death, unless that property is transferred to your spouse. If the property has appreciated during the time you owned it, taxation on capital gains will occur. Registered Retirement Savings Plans (RRSPs) and other similarly structured assets are also included as taxable income unless transferred to a beneficiary as well. Those are just a few examples of how an estate can become subject to a heavy tax burden. The unique benefits of a life insurance policy provide ways to handle this tax burden, solving any liquidity problems that may arise if your family members want to hold onto an illiquid asset, such as a piece of property or an investment. Life insurance can provide a significant amount of money to a family member or other beneficiary, and that money is likely to remain exempt from taxation or seizure.

One of life insurance's most important benefits is that it is not considered part of the estate of the policy holder. The death benefit that is paid by the insurance company goes exclusively to the beneficiaries listed on the policy. This shields the proceeds of the policy from fees and costs that can reduce an estate, including probate proceedings, attorneys' fees and claims made by creditors. The distribution of your life insurance policy is also unaffected by delays of the estate's distribution, like probate. Your beneficiaries will get the proceeds of the policy in a timely fashion, regardless of how long it takes for the rest of your estate to be settled.

Investing a portion of your assets in a life insurance policy can also protect that portion of your estate from creditors. If you owe money to someone or some entity at the time of your death, a creditor is not able to claim any money from a life insurance policy or an annuity, for that matter. As an exception to this rule, if you had already used the life insurance policy as collateral against a loan. If a large portion of the money you want to dedicate to your legacy is sitting in a savings account, investment or other liquid form, creditors may be able to receive their claim on it before your beneficiaries get anything - that is, if there's anything left. A life insurance policy protects your assets from creditors and ensures that your beneficiaries get the money that you intend them to have.

HOW MUCH LIFE INSURANCE DO YOU NEED?

Determining the type of policy and the amount right for you depends on an analysis of your needs. A financial professional can help you complete a needs analysis that will highlight the amount of insurance that you require to meet your goals. This type of personalized review will allow you to determine ways to continue providing income for your spouse or any dependents you may have. A financial professional can also help you calculate the amount of income that your policy should replace to meet the needs of your beneficiaries and the duration of the distribution of that income.

You may also want to use your life insurance policy to meet any expenses associated with your death. These can include funeral costs, fees from probate and legal proceedings, and taxes. You may also want to dedicate a portion of your policy proceeds to help fund tuition or other expenses for your children or grandchildren. You can buy a policy and hope it covers all of those costs, or you can work with a professional who can calculate exactly how much insurance you need and how to structure it to meet your goals. Which would you rather do?

AVOIDING POTENTIAL SNAGS

There are benefits to having life insurance supersede the direction given in a will or other estate plan, but there are also some potential snags that you should address to meet your wishes. For example, if your will instructs that your assets be divided equally between your two children but your life insurance beneficiary is listed as just one of the children, the assets in the life insurance policy will only be distributed to the child listed as the beneficiary. The beneficiary designation of your life insurance supersedes your will's instruction. This is important to understand when designating beneficiaries on a policy you purchase. Work with a professional to make sure that your beneficiaries are accurately listed on your assets, especially your life insurance policies.

USING LIFE INSURANCE TO BUILD YOUR LEGACY

Depending on your goals, there are strategies you can use that could multiply how much you leave behind. Life insurance is one of the most surefire and efficient investment tools for building a substantial legacy that will meet your financial goals.

Here is a brief overview of how life insurance can boost your legacy:

- Life insurance provides an immediate increase in your legacy.
- It provides an income tax-advantaged death benefit for your beneficiaries.

- A good life insurance policy has the opportunity to accumulate value over time.
- It may have an option to include long-term care (LTC) or chronic illness benefits should you require them.

If your Green Money income needs for retirement are met and you have Yellow Money assets that will provide for your future expenses, you may have extra assets that you want to earmark as legacy funds. By electing to invest those assets into a life insurance policy, you can immediately increase the amount of your legacy. Remember, life insurance allows you to transfer a tax-advantaged lump sum of money to your beneficiaries. It remains in your control during your lifetime, can provide for your long- term care needs and bypasses probate costs. And make no mistake, taxes can have a huge impact on your legacy. Not only that, income and assets from your legacy can have tax implications for your beneficiaries, as well.

Here's a brief overview of how taxes could affect your legacy and your beneficiaries:

- The higher your income, the higher the rate at which it is taxed.
- Withdrawals from qualified plans are taxed as income.
- What's more, when you leave a large qualified plan, it ends up being taxed at a high rate.
- If you left a $500,000 IRA to your child, they could end up owing as much as $140,000 in income taxes.
- However, if you could just withdraw $50,000 a year, the tax bill might only be $10,000 per year.

How could you use that annual amount to leave a larger legacy? Luckily, you can leverage a life insurance policy to avoid those tax penalties, preserving a larger amount of your legacy and freeing your beneficiaries from an added tax burden.

» When Brenda turned 70 years old, she decided it was time to look into life insurance policy options. She still feels young, but she remembers that her mother died in early 70s, and she wants to plan ahead so she can pass on some of her legacy to her grandchildren just like her grandmother did for her.

Brenda doesn't really want to think about life insurance, but she does want the security, reliability and tax-advantaged distribution that it offers. She lives modestly, and her Social Security benefit meets most of her income needs. As the beneficiary of her late husband's Certificate of Deposit (CD), she has $100,000 in an account that she has never used and doesn't anticipate ever needing since her income needs were already met.

After looking at several different investment options with a professional, Brenda decides that a Single Premium life insurance policy fits her needs best. She can buy the policy with a $100,000 one-time payment and she is guaranteed that it would provide more than the value of the contract to her beneficiaries. If she left the money in the CD, it would be subject to taxes. But for every dollar that she puts into the life insurance policy, her beneficiaries are guaranteed at least that dollar plus a death benefit, and all of it will be **tax-free!**

For $100,000, Brenda's particular policy offers a $170,000 death benefit distribution to her beneficiaries. By moving the $100,000 from a CD to a life insurance policy, Brenda increases her legacy by 70 percent. Not only that, she has also sheltered it from taxes, so her beneficiaries will be able to receive $1.70 for every $1.00 that she entered into the policy! While buying the policy doesn't allow her to use the money for herself, it does allow her family to benefit from her well-planned legacy.

MAKE YOUR WISHES KNOWN

Estate taxes used to be a much hotter topic in the mid-2000s when the estate tax limits and exclusions were much smaller and taxed at a higher rate than today. In 2008, estates valued at $2 million or more were taxed at 45 percent. Just two years later, the limit was raised to $5 million dollars taxed at 35 percent. The limit has continued to rise ever since. The limit applies to fewer people than before. Estate organization, however, is just as important as ever, and it affects everyone.

Ask yourself:
- Are your assets actually titled and held the way you think they are?
- Are your beneficiaries set up the way you think they should be?
- Have there been changes to your family or those you desire as beneficiaries?

There is more to your legacy beyond your property, money, investments and other assets that you leave to family members, loved ones and charities. Everyone has a legacy beyond money. You also leave behind personal items of importance, your values and beliefs, your personal and family history, and your wishes. Beyond a will and a plan for your assets, it is important that you make your wishes known to someone for the rest of your personal legacy. When it comes time for your family and loved ones to make decisions after you are gone, knowing your wishes can help them make decisions that honor you and your legacy, and give meaning to what you leave behind. Your professional can help you organize.

Think about your:
- Personal stories/recollections
- Values
- Personal items of emotional significance
- Financial assets

- Do you want to make a plan to pass these things on to your family?

WORKING WITH A PROFESSIONAL

Part of using life insurance to your greatest advantage is selecting the policy and provider that can best meet your goals. Venturing into the jungle of policies, brokers and salespeople can be overwhelming, and can leave you wondering if you've made the best decision. Working with a trusted financial professional can help you cut through the red tape, the "sales-speak" and confusion to find a policy that meets your goals and best serves your desires for your money. If you already have a policy, a financial professional can help you review it and become familiar with the policy's premium, the guarantees the policy affords, its performance, and its features and benefits. A financial professional can also help you make any necessary changes to the policy.

> *» When Lettie turned 88, her daughter finally convinced her to meet with a financial professional to help her organize her assets and get her legacy in order. Although Lettie is reluctant to let a stranger in on her personal finances, she ends up very glad that she did.*
>
> *In the process of listing Lettie's assets and her beneficiaries, her professional finds a man's name listed as the beneficiary of an old life insurance annuity that she owns. It turns out, the man is Lettie's ex-husband who is still alive. Had Lettie passed away before her ex-husband, the annuities and any death benefits that came with them, would have been passed on to her ex-husband. This does not reflect her latest wishes.*

Things change, relationships evolve and the way you would like your legacy organized needs to adapt to the changes that happen throughout your life. There may be a new child or grandchild in your family, or you may have been divorced or remarried. A professional will regularly review your legacy assets and ask you questions to make sure that everything is up to date and that the current organization reflects your current wishes.

CHAPTER 12 RECAP //

- You can structure your assets in ways that maximize distributions to your beneficiaries.
- Working with a financial professional can help you select a policy that best meets your needs, fine tune an existing policy, and help you avoid the ponderous and expensive probate process.
- A financial professional can help review the details of the assets you have designated to be a part of your legacy and make sure that you aren't unintentionally disinheriting your heirs.
- Life insurance provides for the distribution of tax-free, liquid assets to your beneficiaries and can significantly build your legacy.
- You can take advantage of a "Stretch IRA" to provide income for you, your spouse and your beneficiaries throughout their lifetimes.
- To avoid unintentional disinheritance, understand the difference between the designations *per stirpes* and *per capita*.

13
YOUR LEGACY BEYOND DOLLARS AND CENTS

"What difference have you made in the lives of others?"

Today, there is more consideration given to planning a legacy than just maximizing your estate. When most people think about an estate, it may seem like something only the very wealthy have: a stately manor or an enormous business. But a legacy is something else entirely. When you get to the end of your life, you may find that a legacy isn't about how much money you made, or the things you have. It's about the difference you made in people's lives.

A legacy encompasses the stories that others tell about you, the shared experiences, and values. An estate may pay for college tuition, but a legacy can inform your grandchildren about the importance of higher education and self-reliance.

A legacy may also contain family heirlooms or items of emotional significance. It may be a piece of art your great-grandmother painted, family photos, or a childhood keepsake.

When you go about planning your legacy, certainly explore strategies that can maximize the financial benefit to the ones you care about. But also take the time to ensure that you have organized the whole of your legacy, and let that be a part of the last gift you leave.

Many people avoid planning their legacy until they feel they must. Something may change in your life, like the birth of a grandchild, the diagnosis of a serious health problem, or the death of a close friend or loved one. Waiting for tragedy to strike in order to get your affairs in order is not the best course of action. The emotional stress of that kind of situation can make it hard to make patient, thoughtful decisions. Taking the time to create a premeditated and thoughtful legacy plan will assure that your assets will be transferred where and when you want them when the time comes.

THE BENEFITS OF PLANNING YOUR LEGACY

The distribution of your assets, whether in the form of property, stocks, Individual Retirement Accounts, 401(k)s or liquid assets, can be a complicated undertaking if you haven't left clear instructions about how you want them handled. Not having a plan will cost more money and take more time, leaving your loved ones to wait (sometimes for years) and receive less of your legacy than if you had a clear plan.

Planning your legacy will help your assets be transferred with little delay and little confusion. Instead of leaving decisions about how to distribute your estate to your family, attorneys or financial professionals, preserve your legacy and your wishes by drafting a clear plan at an early age.

And while you know all that, it can still be hard to sit down and do it. It reminds you that life is short, and the relatively complicated nature of sorting through your assets can feel like a daunting task. But one thing is for sure: *it is impossible for your assets to be transferred or distributed the way you want at the end of your life if you don't have a plan.*

Ask yourself:
- Are my assets up to date?
- Have my primary and contingent beneficiaries been clearly designated?
- Does my plan allow for restriction of a beneficiary?
- Does my legacy plan address minor children that I want to provide with income?
- Does my legacy plan allow for multi-generational payout?

Answers to these questions are critical if you want the final say in how your assets are distributed. In order to achieve your legacy goals, you need a plan.

MAKING A PLAN

Eventually, when your income need is filled and you have sufficient standby money to meet your need for emergencies, travel or other extra expenses you are planning for, whatever isn't used during your lifetime becomes your financial legacy. The money that you do not use during your lifetime will either go to loved ones, unloved ones, charity, or the IRS. The questions is, who would you rather disinherit?

By having a legacy plan that clearly outlines your assets, your beneficiaries and your distribution goals, you can make sure that your money and property is ending up in the hands of the people you determine beforehand. Is it really that big of a deal? It absolutely is. Think about it. Without a clear plan, it is impossible for anyone to know if your beneficiary designations are current and reflect your wishes because you haven't clearly expressed who your beneficiaries are. You may have an idea of who you want your assets to go to, but without a plan, it is anyone's guess. It is also impossible to know if the titling of your assets is accurate unless you have gone through and determined whose name is on the titles. More importantly, *if you have not clearly and effectively communicated your desires regarding the planned distribution of your legacy, you and your family may end up losing a large part of it.*

As you can see, managing a legacy is more complicated than having an attorney read your will, divide your estate and write checks to your heirs. The additional issue of taxes, Family Maximum Benefit calculations and a host of other decisions rear their heads. Educating yourself about the best options for positioning your legacy assets is a challenging undertaking. Working with a financial professional who is versed in determining the most efficient and effective ways of preserving and distributing your legacy can save you time, money and strife.

So, how do you begin?

Making a Legacy Plan Starts with a Simple List. The first, and one of the largest, steps to setting up an estate plan with a financial professional that reflects your desires is creating a detailed inventory of your assets and debts (if you have any). You need to know what assets you have, who the beneficiaries are, how much they are worth and how they are titled. You can start by identifying and listing your assets. This is a good starting point for working with a financial professional who can then help you determine the detailed information about your assets that will dictate how they are distributed upon your death.

If you are particularly concerned about leaving your kids and grandkids a lifetime of income with minimal taxes, you will want to discuss a Stretch IRA option with your financial professional.

STRETCH IRAS: GETTING THE MOST OUT OF YOUR MONEY

In 1986, the U.S. Congress passed a law that allows for multi-generational distributions of IRA assets. This type of distribution is called a Stretch IRA because it stretches the distribution of the account out over a longer period of time to several beneficiaries. It also allows the account to continue accumulating value throughout your relatives' lifetimes. You can use a Stretch IRA as an income tool that distributes throughout your lifetime, your children's lifetimes and your grandchildren's lifetimes.

Stretch IRAs are an attractive option for those more concerned with creating income for their loved ones than leaving them with a lump sum that may be subject to a high tax rate. With traditional IRA distributions, non-spousal beneficiaries must generally take distributions from their inherited IRAs, whether transferred or not, within five years after the death of the IRA owner. An exception to this rule applies if the beneficiary elects to take distributions over his or her lifetime, which is referred to as stretching the IRA.

Let's begin by looking at the potential of stretching an IRA throughout multiple generations.

> » *In this scenario, Mr. Cleaver has an IRA with a current balance of $350,000. If we assume a five percent annual rate of return, and a 28% tax rate, the Stretch IRA turned a $502,625 legacy into more than $1.5 million. Doubling the value of the IRA also provided Mr. Cleaver, his wife, two children and three grandchildren with income. Not choosing the stretch option would have cost nearly $800,000 and had impacts on six of Mr. Cleaver's loved ones.*

Unfortunately, many things may also play a role in failing to stretch IRA distributions. It can be tempting for a beneficiary to take a lump sum of money despite the tax consequences. Fortunately, if you want to solidify your plan for distribution, there are options that will allow you to open up an IRA and incorporate "spendthrift" clauses for your beneficiaries. This will ensure your legacy is stretched appropriately and to your specifications. Only certain insurance companies allow this option, and you will not find this benefit with any brokerage accounts. You need to work with a financial professional who has the appropriate relationship with an insurance company that provides this option.

CHAPTER 13 RECAP //

- Your legacy encompasses more than just the physical assets left behind for your children. It encompasses the ideals and values important to you.
- Managing a legacy is more complicated than having an attorney read your will, divide your estate, and write checks to your heirs. Issue such as taxes, Family Maximum Benefit calculations and a host of other concerns make it necessary to educate yourself. Working with a financial professional can save you time, money and stress.
- Legacy planning begins with a simple list.

14
CHOOSING A FINANCIAL PROFESSIONAL

From the moment you dip your toes into the retirement planning pool to the point you start swimming laps, your assets organized, your income needs met, and your accumulation and legacy plans in place, working with a professional that you trust can make all the difference in how well your retirement reflects your desires.

It is important to know what you are looking for before taking the plunge. There are many people that would love to handle your money, but not everyone is qualified to handle it in a way that leads to a holistic approach to creating a solid retirement plan.

The distinction being made here is that you should look for someone that puts your interests first and actively wants to help you meet your goals and objectives. Oftentimes, the products someone sells you matter less than their dedication to making sure that you have a plan that meets your needs.

Professionals take your whole financial position into consideration. They make plans that adjust your risk exposure, invest in tools that secure your desired income during retirement and create investment strategies that allow you to continue accumulating wealth during your retirement for you to use later or to contribute to your legacy. If you buy stocks with a broker, use a different agent for a life insurance policy and have an unmanaged 401(k) through your employer, working with a financial professional will consolidate the management of your assets so you have one trustworthy person quarterbacking all of the team elements of your portfolio. Financial products and investment tools change, but the concepts that lie behind wise retirement planning are lasting. In the end, a financial professional's approach is designed for those serious about planning for retirement. *Can you say the same thing about the person that advises you about your financial life?*

It's easy to see how choosing a financial professional can be one of the most important decisions you can make in your life. Not only do they provide you with advice, they also manage the personal assets that supply your retirement income and contribute to your legacy. So, how do you find a good one?

HOW TO FIND A FINANCIAL PROFESSIONAL YOU CAN TRUST

Taking care to select a financial professional is one of the best things you can do for yourself and for your future. Your professional has influence and control of your investment decisions, making their role in your life more than just important. Your financial security and the quality of your retirement depends on the decisions, investment strategies and asset structuring that you and your professional create.

Working with a professional is different than calling up a broker when you want to buy or trade some stock. This isn't a decision that you can hand off to anyone else. You need to bring your time and attention to the table when it comes to finding someone with whom you can entrust your financial life. Separating the wheat from the chaff will take some work, but you'll be happy you did it.

While no one can tell you exactly who to choose or how to choose them, the following information can help you narrow the field:

- You can start by asking your friends, family and colleagues for referrals. You will want to pay particular attention to the recommendations that you get from others who are in your similar financial situation and who have similar lifestyle choices. The professional for the CEO of your company may have a different skill-set than the skill-set of the professional befitting your cousin who has 3 kids and a Subaru like you. Do follow-up research on the Internet as well. Look up the people who have been recommended to you on websites like LinkedIn that show the work history, referrals and experience of the candidates that you find most attractive. You will also learn about the firms with or for whom they work. The investment philosophies and reputations of the companies they work for will tell you a lot about how they will handle your money.

- The other side of the coin, however, is that everyone and their brother has a recommendation about how you should manage your money and who should manage it for you. From hot stock tips to "the best money manager in the state," people love to share good information that makes them look like they are in-the-know. Nobody wants to talk about the bad stock purchases they made, the times they lost money and the poor selections they made regarding financial professionals or stock brokers. If you decide to take a friend or family member's recommendation, make sure they have a substantial, long-term experience with the financial professional and that their glowing review isn't just based on a one-time "win."

- You can also use online tools like the search function of the Financial Planning Association (http://www.fpanet.org/) and the National Association of Personal Financial Advisors (http://www.napfa.org/). Most of the professionals listed on these sites do not earn commissions from selling financial products, but are instead paid on a fee-only basis for their services. It is important to understand how your professional is being paid. It is generally considered preferable to work with a fee-based professional who will not have conflicts of interests between earning a commission and acting in your best interests.
- Many professionals may also be brokers or dealers that can earn commissions on things like life insurance, certain types of annuities and disability insurance. These professionals have most likely intentionally overlapped their roles so that if their clients choose to purchase insurance or investment products that require a broker or dealer, those clients won't have to find an additional person to work with. Again, understanding the role of your professional will help you make your determination.

NARROWING THE FIELD

1. Decide on the Type of Professional with Whom You Want to Work. There are four basic kinds of financial professionals. Many professionals may play overlapping roles. It is important to know a professional's primary function, how they charge for their services and whether they are obligated to act in your best interest.

Registered representatives, better known as stockbrokers or bank/investment representatives, make their living by earning commissions on insurance products and investment services. Stockbrokers basically sell you things. The products from which they make the highest commission are sometimes the products that they recommend to their clients. If you want to make a simple transaction, such as buying or selling a particular stock, a registered representative can help you. Although registered representatives are licensed professionals, if you want to create a structured and planful approach to positioning your assets for retirement, you might want to consider continuing your search.

The term "planner" is often misused. It can refer to credible professionals that are CPAs, CFPs and ChFCs to your uncle's next door neighbor who claims to have a lead on some undervalued stock about to be "discovered." A wide array of people may claim to be planners because there are no requirements to be a planner. The term financial planner, however, refers to someone who is properly registered as an investment advisor and serves as a fiduciary as described below.

Financial professionals are the diamonds in the rough. These Registered Investment Advisors are compensated on a fee basis. They do, however, often have licensure as stockbrokers or insurance agents, allowing them to earn commissions on certain transactions. More importantly, **financial professionals are financial fiduciaries, meaning they are required to make financial decisions in your best interest and reflecting your risk tolerance.** Investment Advisors are held to high ethical standards and are highly regarded in the financial industry. Financial professionals also often take a more comprehensive approach to asset management. These professionals are trained and credentialed to plan and coordinate their clients' assets in order to meet their goals or retirement and legacy planning. They are not focused on individual stocks, investments or markets. They look at the big picture, the whole enchilada.

Money managers are on par with financial professionals. However, they are often given explicit permission to make investment decisions without advanced approval by their clients.

Understanding who you are working with and what their title is the first step to planning your retirement. While each of the above-mentioned types of financial professionals can help you with aspects of your finances, it is **financial professionals** who have the most intimate role, the most objective investment strategies and the most unbiased mode of compensation for their services. A financial professional can also help you with the non-financial aspects of your legacy and can help you find ways to create a tax planning strategy to help you save money.

2. Be Objective. At the end of the day, you need to separate the weak from the strong. While you might want a strong personal rapport with your professional, or you may want to choose your professional for their personality and positive attitude, it is more important that you find someone who will give sage advice regarding achieving your retirement goals.

It can be helpful to use a process of elimination to narrow the field of potential professionals. Look into five or six potential leads and cross off your list the ones that don't meet your requirements until only one or two remain. Cross-check your remaining choices against the list of things you need from a professional. Make sure they represent a firm that has the investment tools and products that you desire, and make sure they have experience in retirement planning. That is, after all, the main goal.

Don't be afraid to investigate each of your candidates. You'll want to ask the same questions and look for the same information from everyone you consider so you can then compare them and discern which is best for you. You'll want to take a look at the specific credentials of each professional, their experience and competence, their ethics and fiduciary status, their history and track record, and a list of the services that they offer. The professionals who meet all or most of your qualifications are the ones you will contact for an interview.

Potential professionals should meet your qualifications in the following categories:

- *Credentials:* Look at their experience, the quality of their education, any associations to which they belong and certifications they have earned. Someone who has continued their professional education through ongoing certifications will be more up-to-date on current financial practices compared to someone who got their degree 25 years ago and hasn't done a thing since.
- *Practices:* Look at the track record of your candidates, how they are compensated for their services, the reports and analysis they offer, and their value added services.
- *Services:* Your professional must meet your needs. If you are planning your retirement, you should work with someone who offers services that help you to that end. You want someone who can offer planning, advice on investment strategies, ways to calculate risk, advice on insurance and annuities products, and ways to manage your tax strategy.
- *Ethics:* You want to work with someone who is above board and does things the right way. Vet them by checking their compliance record, current licensing, fiduciary status and, yes, even their criminal record. You never know!

3. Ask for and Check References. Once you have selected two or three professionals that you want to meet, call or email them and ask for references. Every professional should be able to provide you with at least two or three names. In fact, they will probably be eager to share them with you. Most professionals rely on references for validation of their success, quality of services and likability. You should, however, take them with a grain of salt. You have no way to know whether or not references are a professional's friends or colleagues.

It is worth contacting references, however, to check for inconsistencies. Ask each reference the same set of questions to get the same basic information. How long have they been working with the professional? What kind of services have they used and were they happy with them? What type of financial planning did they use the professional for? Were they versed in the type of financial planning that you needed? You can also ask them direct questions to elicit candid responses. What was the full cost of the expenses that your professional charged you? Do the reports and statements you receive come from the same firm? Questions like these can help you get a sense of how well the reference knows their professional and whether or not they are a quality reference.

A good reference is a bit like icing on the cake. It's nice to have them, but nothing speaks louder than a good track record and quality experience. And remember that a good reference, while nice to hear, is relatively cheap. How many times have you heard someone on the golf course or at work telling you how great their stockbroker is? But how many times have you heard about the bad investments or losses they have experienced?

4. Use the Internet. As a final step before picking up the phone and calling your candidates, do some digging to discover if anyone on your list has a history of unlawful or unethical practices, or has been disciplined for any of their professional behavior or decisions. Don't worry, you don't have to hire a private investigator. You can easily find this information on the Financial Industry Regulatory Authority's (FINRA) online BrokerCheck tool at: http://www.finra.org/Investors/ToolsCalculators/BrokerCheck/.

You can also look up Registered Investment Advisory Firms and Individuals using the SEC's search tool at: http://www.adviserinfo.sec.gov.

You should obviously explore the website of a potential professional and the website of the firm that they represent. The Internet allows you to go beyond the online business card of a professional to gain access to information that they don't control. It may all be good information! Or a brief search of the Internet could reveal a sketchy past. The best part is that the Internet allows you to find helpful information in an anonymous fashion.

Start with Google (www.google.com) and search the name of a potential professional and their firm. Keep your eyes trained on third party sources such as articles, blog posts or news stories that mention the professional. You can also check a professional's compliance records online with the Financial Industry Regulatory Authority (FINRA) and the Securities and Exchange Commission (SEC). If you want to dig deeper, you can combine search terms like "scams," "lawsuits," "suspensions" and "fraud" with a professional's or firm's name to see what information arises. More likely than not, you won't find anything. But if you do, you'll be glad that you checked.

HOW TO INTERVIEW CANDIDATES

After vetting your candidates and narrowing down a list of professionals that you think might be a good fit for you, it's time to start interviewing.

When you meet in person with a professional, you want to take advantage of your time with them. The presentations and information that they share with you will be important to pay attention to, but you will also want to control some aspects of the interview. After a professional has told you what they want you to hear, it's time to ask your own questions to get the specific information you need to make your decision.

Make sure to prepare a list of questions and an informal agenda so that you can keep track of what you want to ask and what points you want the professional to touch on during the interview. Using the same questions and agenda will also allow you to more easily compare the professionals after you have interviewed them all. Remember that these interviews are just that, *interviews*. You are meeting with several professionals to determine with whom you want to work. Don't agree to anything or sign anything during an interview until after you have made your final decision.

It can also be helpful to put a time limit on your interviews and to meet the professionals at their offices. The time limit will keep things on track and will allow structured time for presentations and questions/discussion. By meeting them at their office, you can get a sense of the work environment, the staff culture and attitude, and how the firm does business. If you are unable to travel to a professional's office and must meet them at your home or office, make sure that your interviews are scheduled with plenty of time between so the professionals don't cross each other's paths.

You can use the following questions during an initial interview to get an understanding of how each professional does business and whether they are a good fit for you:

1. How do you charge for your services? How much do you charge? This information should be easy to find on their website, but if you don't see it, ask. Find out if they charge an initial planning fee, if they charge a percentage for assets under their management and if they make money by selling specific financial products or services. If so, you should follow up by asking how much the service costs. This will give you an idea of how they really make their money and if they have incentive to sell certain products over others. Make sure you understand exactly how you will be charged so there are no surprises down the road if you decide to work with this person.

2. What are your credentials, licenses, and certifications? There are Certified Financial Planners (CFPs), Chartered Financial Consultants (ChFCs), Investment Advisor Representatives, Certified Public Accountants (CPAs) and Personal Financial Specialists (PFSs). Whatever their credentials or titles, you want to be sure that the professional you work with is an expert in the field relevant to your circumstances. If you want someone to manage your money, you will most likely look for an Investment Advisor. Someone that works with an independent firm will likely have a team of CPAs, CFPs and other financial experts upon whom they can draw. If you like the professional you are meeting with and you think they might be a good fit, but they don't have the accounting experience you want them to have, ask about their firm and the resources available to them. If they work closely with CPAs that are experienced in your needs, it could be a good match.

3. What are the financial services that you and your firm provide? The question within the question here is, "Can you help me achieve my goals?" Some people can only provide you with investment advice, and others are tax consultants. You will likely want to work with someone that provides a complete suite of financial planning services and products that touch on retirement planning, insurance options, legacy and estate structuring, and tax planning. Whatever services they provide, make sure they meet your needs and your anticipated needs.

4. What kinds of clients do you work with the most? A lot of financial professionals work within a niche: retirement planning, risk assessment, life insurance, etc. Finding someone who works with other people that are in the same financial boat as you and who have similar goals can be an important way to make sure they understand your needs. While someone might be a crackerjack annuities cowboy, you might not be interested in that option. Ask follow-up questions that will really help you understand where their expertise lies and whether or not their experience lines up with your needs.

5. May I see a sample of one of your financial plans? You wouldn't buy a car without test driving it, and you should not work with a professional without seeing a sample of how they do business. While there is no formal structure that a financial plan has to follow, the variation between professionals can help you find someone who "speaks your language." One professional may provide you with an in-depth analysis that relies heavily on info graphics and diagrams. Someone else may give you a seven page review of your assets and general recommendations. By seeing a sample plan, you can narrow down who presents information in the way that you desire and in ways that you understand.

6. How do you approach investing? You may be entirely in the dark about how to approach your investments, or you might have some guiding principles. Either way, ask each candidate what their philosophy is. Some will resonate with you and some won't. A good professional who has a realistic approach to investing won't promise you the moon or tell you that they can make you a lot of money. Professionals who are successful at retirement planning and full service financial management will tell you that they will listen to your goals, risk tolerance and comfort level with different types of investment strategies. Working with someone that you trust is critical, and this question in particular can help you find out who you can and who you can't.

7. How do you remain in contact with your clients? Does your prospective professional hold annual, quarterly or monthly meetings? How often do *you* want to meet with your professional? Some people want to check in once a year, go over everything and make sure their ducks are all in a row. If any changes over the previous year or additions to their legacy planning strategy came up, they'll do it on that date. Other people want a monthly update to be more involved in the decision making process and to understand what's happening with their portfolio. You basically need to determine the right degree of involvement for both you and your financial professional. You'll also want to feel out how your professional communicates. Do you prefer phone calls or face-to-face meetings? Do you want your professional to explain things to you in detail or to summarize for you what decisions they've made? Is the professional willing to give you their direct phone number or their email address? More importantly, do you want that information and do you want to be able to contact them in those ways?

8. Are you my main contact, or do you work with a team? This is another way of finding out how involved with you your professional will be, and how often they will meet with you. It is also a way to discover how the firm they represent operates and manages their clients. Some professionals will answer their own phone, meet with you regularly and have your home phone number on speed dial. Others will meet with you once a year and have a partner or assistant check in with you every quarter to give you an update. Other companies take an entirely team-based approach whereby clients have a main contact but their portfolio is handled by a team of professionals that represent the firm. One way isn't better than another, but one way will be best for you. Find out how the professional you are interviewing operates before entering into an agreement.

9. How do you provide a unique experience for your clients? This is a polite way of asking, "Why should I work with you?" A professional should have a compelling answer to this question that connects with you. Their answer will likely touch on their investment philosophy, their communication style and their expertise. If you hear them describing strengths and philosophies that resonate with you, keep them on your list. Some professionals will tell you that they will make investments with your money that match your values, others will say they will maximize your returns and others will say they will protect your capital while structuring your assets for income. Whatever you're looking for in a professional, you will most likely find it in the answer to this question.

This last question you will want to ask *yourself* after you've met with someone who you are considering hiring:

10. Did they ask questions and show signs that they were interested in working with me? A professional who will structure your assets to reflect your risk tolerance and to position you for a comfortable retirement must be a good listener. You will want to pass by a professional who talks non-stop and tells you what to do without listening to what you want them to do. If you felt they listened well and understood your needs, and seemed interested and experienced in your situation, then they might be right for you.

THE IMPORTANCE OF INDEPENDENCE

Not all investment firms and financial professionals are created equal. The information in this book has systematically shown that leveraging investments for income and accumulation in today's market requires new ideas and modern planning. In short, you need innovative ideas to come up with the creative solutions that will provide you with the retirement that you want. Innovation thrives on independence. No matter how good a financial professional is, the firm that they represent needs to operate on principles that make sense in today's economy. Remember, advice about money has been around forever. Good advice, however, changes with the times.

CHOOSING A FINANCIAL PROFESSIONAL

Timing the market, relying on the sale of stocks for income and banking on high treasury and bond returns are not strategies. They aren't even realistic ways to make money or to generate income. Working with an independent agent can help you break free from the old ways of thinking and position you to create a realistic retirement plan.

Working with an independent professional who relies on fee-based income tied to the success of their performance will also give you greater peace of mind. When you do well, they do well, and that's the way it should be. Your independent financial professional will make sure that:

- Your assets are organized and structured to reflect your risk tolerance.
- Your assets will be available to you when you need them and in the way that you need them.
- You will have a lifetime income that will support your lifestyle through your retirement.
- You are handling your taxes as efficiently as possible.
- Your legacy is in order.
- Your Red Money is turned into Yellow Money, and is managed in your best interest.

> *» Remember Jack and Beverly from Chapter 1? Even though they knew they had Social Security benefits coming, they placed some money in savings and each had a pension or a 401(k).* ***Before they met with a financial professional, they had no idea what their retirement would look like.*** *After they met with an agent, they knew exactly what types of assets they had, how much they were worth, how much risk they were exposed to and how they were going to be distributed. They also created an income plan so that they could pay their bills every month the moment they retired, and they maximized their Social Security benefit by targeting the year*

and month they would get the most lifetime benefits. After their income needs were met, they were able to continue accumulating wealth by investing their extra assets to serve them in the future and contribute to their legacy. Their professional also helped them make decisions that impacted their taxes, protecting the value of their assets and allowing them to keep more of their money.

*This isn't a fairy tale scenario. This is an example of how much you stand to gain by meeting with a financial professional who can help you create a planful approach to your retirement. The concept of Know So and Hope So didn't just apply to their money, it also applied to Jack and Beverly. They **hoped** that they would have enough for retirement and that they had worked hard enough and saved enough to maintain their lifestyle. Working with a financial professional allowed them to **know** that their income needs were secured and structured to provide them with income for the rest of their lives and with some money to spare.*

Now, ask yourself: Is your retirement built on hopes and dreams, or a solid, predictable plan?

IT'S WORTH IT!

Finding, interviewing and selecting a financial professional can seem like a daunting task. And honestly, it will take a good amount of work to narrow the field and find the one you want. In the end, it is worth the blood, sweat and tears. Your retirement, lifestyle, assets and legacy is on the line. The choices you make today will have lasting impacts on your life and the life of your loved ones. Working with someone you trust and know you can rely on to make decisions that will benefit you is invaluable. The work it takes to find them is something you will never regret.

Here is a recap of why working with a financial professional is the best retirement decision you can make:

CHAPTER 14 RECAP //

- If you feel you have more *Hope So* than *Know So* about your money and what your retirement is going to look like, working with a financial professional will give you clarity and confidence about what decisions are best for you.
- It is difficult for individual investors to not make emotional decisions about their investments. Financial professionals work with your risk tolerance, income needs and assets to find the most logical, efficient and beneficial way for you to structure your investments.
- As the DALBAR report showed, a majority of individual investors sell low when the market goes down and buy high when it goes back up. This is literally the exact opposite of what they should do to maximize their returns.
- A financial professional can help you change strategies when the market isn't going your way, but they won't abandon ship. They will stick to a planful approach.
- Yellow Money is different from a mutual fund or a 401(k) because, while funds and 401(k)s are investment tools, they are not investment strategies. A 401(k) can be particularly misconceiving because your employer isn't truly structuring your investments inside the 401(k). They are simply providing you with a few options. The same goes for mutual funds. They are not truly managed by someone who is obligated to have your best interests and your risk tolerance in mind.
- The biggest difference between working with a financial professional to manage your funds, and buying a mutual fund is that, while a mutual fund buys 20 stocks and pegs its earnings on the overall performance of the portfolio, a financial professional works with you to create an overall financial strategy that meets your needs.

- Not all investment firms and financial professionals are created equal. Working with an independent professional will give you more options that are customizable to your life.

GLOSSARY

ANNUAL RESET *(ANNUAL RATCHET, CLIQUET)* – Crediting methods measuring index movement over a one year period. Positive interest is calculated and credited at the end of each contract year and cannot be lost if the index subsequently declines. Say that the index increased from 100 to 110 in one year and the indexed annuity had an 80 percent participation rate. The insurance company would take the 10 percent gross index gain for the year (110-100/100), apply the participation rate (10 percent index gain x 80 percent rate) and credit 8 percent interest to the annuity. But, what if in the following year the index declined back to 100? The individual would keep the 8 percent interest earned and simply receive zero interest for the down year. An annual reset structure preserves credited gains and treats negative index periods as years with zero growth.

ANNUITANT – The person, usually the annuity owner, whose life expectancy is used to calculate the income payment amount on the annuity.

ANNUITY – An annuity is a contract issued by an insurance company that often serves as a type of savings plan used by individuals looking for long term growth and protection of assets that will likely be needed within retirement.

AVERAGING – Index values may either be measured from a start point to an end point (point-to-point) or values between the start point and end point may be averaged to determine an ending value. Index values may be averaged over the days, weeks, months or quarters of the period.

BENEFICIARY – A beneficiary is the person designated to receive payments due upon the death of the annuity owner or the annuitant themselves.

BONUS RATE – A bonus rate is the "extra" or "additional" interest paid during the first year (the initial guarantee period), typically used as an added incentive to get consumers to select their annuity policy over another.

CALL OPTION (ALSO SEE PUT OPTION) – Gives the holder the right to buy an underlying security or index at a specified price on or before a given date.

CAP – The maximum interest rate that will be credited to the annuity for the year or period. The cap usually refers to the maximum interest credited after applying the participation rate or yield spread. If the index methodology showed a 20 percent increase, the participation rate was 60 percent and the maximum interest cap was 10 percent, the contract would credit 10 percent interest. A few annuities use a maximum gain cap instead of a maximum interest cap with the participation rate or yield spread applied to the lesser of the gain or the cap. If the index methodology showed a 20 percent increase, the participation rate was 60 percent and the maximum gain cap was 10 percent, the contract would credit 6 percent interest.

COMPOUND INTEREST – Interest is earned on both the original principal and on previously earned interest. It is more favorable than simple interest. Suppose that your original principal was $1 and your interest rate was 10 percent for five years. With simple interest, your value is ($1 + $0.10 interest each year) = $1.50. With compound interest, your value is ($1 x 1.10 x 1.10 x 1.10 x 1.10 x 1.10) = $1.61. The advantage of compound interest over simple interest becomes greater as each subsequent period passes.

CREDITING METHOD *(ALSO SEE METHODOLOGY)* – The formula(s) used to determine the excess interest that is credited above the minimum interest guarantee.

DEATH BENEFITS – The payment the annuity owner's estate or beneficiaries will receive if he or she dies before the annuity matures. On most annuities, this is equal to the current account value. Some annuities offer an enhanced value at death via an optional rider that has a monthly or annual fee associated with it.

EXCESS INTEREST – Interest credited to the annuity contract above the minimum guaranteed interest rate. In an indexed annuity the excess interest is determined by applying a stated crediting method to a specific index or indices.

FIXED ANNUITY – A contract issued by an insurance company guaranteeing a minimum interest rate with the crediting of excess interest determined by the performance of the insurer's general account. Index annuities are fixed annuities.

FIXED DEFERRED ANNUITY – With fixed annuities, an insurance company offers a guaranteed interest rate plus safety of your principal and earnings ((subject to the claims-paying ability of the insurance company). Your interest rate will be reset periodically, based on economic and other factors, but is guaranteed to never fall below a certain rate.

FREE WITHDRAWALS – Withdrawals that are free of surrender charges.

INDEX – The underlying external benchmark upon which the crediting of excess interest is based, also a measure of the prices of a group of securities.

IRA *(INDIVIDUAL RETIREMENT ACCOUNT)* – An IRA is a tax-advantaged personal savings plan that lets an individual set aside money for retirement. All or part of the participant's contributions may be tax deductible, depending on the type of IRA chosen and the participant's personal financial circumstances. Distributions from many employer-sponsored retirement plans may be eligible to be rolled into an IRA to continue tax-deferred growth until the funds are needed. An annuity can be used as an IRA; that is, IRA funds can be used to purchase an annuity.

IRA ROLLOVER – IRA rollover is the phrase used when an individual who has a balance in an employer-sponsored retirement plan transfers that balance into an IRA. Such an exchange, when properly handled, is a tax-advantaged transaction.

LIQUIDITY – The ease with which an asset is convertible to cash. An asset with high liquidity provides flexibility, in that the owner can easily convert it to cash at any time, but it also tends to decrease profitability.

GLOSSARY

MARKET RISK – The risk of the market value of an asset fluctuating up or down over time. In a fixed or fixed indexed annuity, the original principal and credited interest are not subject to market risk. Even if the index declines, the annuity owner would receive no less than their original principal back if they decided to cash in the policy at the end of the surrender period. Unlike a security, indexed annuities guarantee the original premium and the premium is backed by, and is as safe as, the insurance company that issued it (subject to the claims-paying ability of the insurance company).

METHODOLOGY *(ALSO SEE CREDITING METHOD)* – The way that interest crediting is calculated. On fixed indexed annuities, there are a variety of different methods used to determine how index movement becomes interest credited.

MINIMUM GUARANTEED RETURN *(MINIMUM INTEREST RATE)* – Fixed indexed annuities typically provide a minimum guaranteed return over the life of the contract. At the time that the owner chooses to terminate the contract, the cash surrender value is compared to a second value calculated using the minimum guaranteed return and the higher of the two values is paid to the annuity owner.

OPTION – A contract which conveys to its holder the right, but not the obligation, to buy or sell something at a specified price on or before a given date. After this given date the option ceases to exist. Insurers typically buy options to provide for the excess interest potential. Options may be American style whereby they may be exercised at any time prior to the given date, or they may have to be exercised only during a specified window. Options that may only be exercised during a specified period are European-style options.

OPTION RISK – Most insurers create the potential for excess interest in an indexed annuity by buying options. Say that you could buy a share of stock for $50. If you bought the stock and it rose to $60 you could sell it and net a $10 profit. But, if the stock price fell to $40 you'd have a $10 loss. Instead of buying the actual stock, we could buy an option that gave us the right to buy the stock for $50 at any time over the next year. The cost of the option is $2. If the stock price rose to $60 we would exercise our option, buy the stock at $50 and make $10 (less the $2 cost of the option). If the price of the stock fell to $40, $30 or $10, we wouldn't use the option and it would expire. The loss is limited to $2 – the cost of the option.

PARTICIPATION RATE – The percentage of positive index movement credited to the annuity. If the index methodology determined that the index increased 10 percent and the indexed annuity participated in 60 percent of the increase, it would be said that the contract has a 60 percent participation rate. Participation rates may also be expressed as asset fees or yield spreads.

POINT-TO-POINT – A crediting method measuring index movement from an absolute initial point to the absolute end point for a period. An index had a period starting value of 100 and a period ending value of 120. A point-to-point method would record a positive index movement of 20 [120-100] or a 20 percent positive movement [(120-100)/100]. Point-to-point usually refers to annual periods; however the phrase is also used instead of term end point to refer to multiple year periods.

PREMIUM BONUS – A premium bonus is additional money that is credited to the accumulation account of an annuity policy under certain conditions.

PUT OPTION *(ALSO SEE CALL OPTION)* – Gives the holder the right to sell an underlying security or index at a specified price on or before a given date.

QUALIFIED ANNUITIES *(QUALIFIED MONEY)* – Qualified annuities are annuities purchased for funding an IRA, 403(b) tax-deferred annuity or other type of retirement arrangements. An IRA or qualified retirement plan provides the tax deferral. An annuity contract should be used to fund an IRA or qualified retirement plan to benefit from an annuity's features other than tax deferral, including the safety features, lifetime income payout option and death benefit protection.

REQUIRED MINIMUM DISTRIBUTION *(RMD)* – The amount of money that Traditional, SEP and SIMPLE IRA owners and qualified plan participants must begin distributing from their retirement accounts by April 1 following the year they reach age 70.5. RMD amounts must then be distributed each subsequent year.

RETURN FLOOR – Another way of saying minimum guaranteed return.

ROTH IRA – Like other IRA accounts, the Roth IRA is simply a holding account that manages your stocks, bonds, annuities, mutual funds and CD's. However, future withdrawals (including earnings and interest) are typically tax-advantaged once the account has been open for five years and the account holder is age 59.5.

RULE OF 72 – Tells you approximately how many years it takes a sum to double at a given rate. It's handy to be able to figure out, without using a calculator, that when you're earning a 6 percent return, for example, by dividing 6 percent into 72, you'll find that it takes 12 years for money to double. Conversely, if you know it took a sum twelve years to double you could divide 12 into 72 to determine the annual return (6 percent).

SIMPLE INTEREST *(ALSO SEE COMPOUND INTEREST)* – Interest is only earned on the original principal.

SPLIT ANNUITY – A split annuity is the term given to an effective strategy that utilizes two or more different annuity products – one designed to generate monthly income and the other to restore the original starting principal over a set period of time.

STANDARD & POOR'S 500 *(S&P 500)* – The most widely used external index by fixed indexed annuities. Its objective is to be a benchmark to measure and report overall U.S. stock market performance. It includes a representative sample of 500 common stocks from companies trading on the New York Stock Exchange, American Stock Exchange, and NASDAQ National Market System. The index represents the price or market value of the underlying stocks and does not include the value of reinvested dividends of the underlying stocks.

STOCK MARKET INDEX – A report created from a type of statistical measurement that shows up or down changes in a specific financial market, usually expressed as points and as a percentage, in a number of related markets, or in an economy as a whole (i.e. S&P 500 or New York Stock Exchange).

SURRENDER CHARGE – A charge imposed for withdrawing funds or terminating an annuity contract prematurely. There is no industry standard for surrender charges, that is, each annuity product has its own unique surrender charge schedule. The charge is usually expressed as a percentage of the amount withdrawn prematurely from the contract. The percentage tends to decline over time, ultimately becoming zero.

TRADITIONAL IRA – See IRA (Individual Retirement Account)

TERM END POINT – Crediting methods measuring index movements over a greater timeframe than a year or two. The opposite of an annual reset method. Also referred to as a term point-to-point method. Say that the index value was at 100 on the first day of the period. If the calculated index value was at 150 at the end of the period the positive index movement would be 50 percent (150-100/100). The company would credit a percentage of this movement as excess interest. Index movement is calculated and interest credited at the end of the term and interim movements during the period are ignored.

TERM HIGH POINT *(HIGH WATER MARK)* – A type of term end point structure that uses the highest anniversary index level as the end point. Say that the index value was at 100 on the first day of the period, reached a value of 160 at the end of a contract year during the period, and ended the period at 150. A term high point method would use the 160 value – the highest contract anniversary point reached during the period, as the end point and the gross index gain would be 60 percent (160-100/100). The company would then apply a participation rate to the gain.

TERM YIELD SPREAD – A type of term end point structure which calculates the total index gain for a period, computes the annual compound rate of return deducts a yield spread from the annual rate of return and then recalculates the total index gain for the period based on the net annual rate. Say that an index increased from 100 to 200 by the end of a nine year period. This is the equivalent of an 8 percent compound annual interest rate. If the annuity had a 2 percent term yield spread this would be deducted from the annual interest rate (8 percent-2 percent) and the net rate would be credited to the contract (6 percent) for each of the nine years. Total index gain may also be computed by using the highest anniversary index level as the end point.

VARIABLE ANNUITY – A contract issued by an insurance company offering separate accounts invested in a wide variety of stocks and/or bonds. The investment risk is borne by the annuity owner. Variable annuities are considered securities and require appropriate securities registration.

1035 EXCHANGE – The 1035 exchange refers to the section of tax code that allows annuity owners the flexibility to exchange one annuity for another without incurring any immediate tax liabilities. This action is most often utilized when an annuity holder decides they want to upgrade an annuity to a more favorable one, but they do not want to activate unnecessary tax liabilities that would typically be encountered when surrendering an existing annuity contract.

401(K) ROLLOVER – See IRA Rollover

GLOSSARY

Made in the USA
Charleston, SC
03 May 2014